ONE-POT
BEST-EVER ONE-POT RECIPES

ONE-POT
BEST-EVER ONE-POT RECIPES

bay books

MEAL PLANNER

Use the following table to plan your best-ever One-pot meal. The recipes have been grouped into appropriate classifications and the portion size of each recipe is clearly shown. Plan your meal and then turn to the appropriate page to find your clear and concise recipe together with a large-format picture of the finished dish.

BEEF, LAMB & PORK

CHICKEN & POULTRY

INGREDIENTS

1 onion, halved
2 cloves
1 carrot, cut into chunks
1 bay leaf
500 g (1 lb) chicken breast fillets
$1/_3$ cup (75 g/$2^1/_2$ oz) short-grain rice
3 eggs, separated
$1/_4$ cup (60 ml/2 fl oz) lemon juice
2 tablespoons chopped fresh flat-leaf parsley
4 thin lemon slices, to garnish

1 Stud the onion halves with the cloves and place in a large saucepan with 1.5 litres (3 pints) water. Add the carrot, bay leaf and chicken. Season with salt and freshly ground black pepper. Slowly bring to the boil, then reduce the heat and simmer for 10 minutes, or until the chicken is cooked.

2 Strain the stock into a clean saucepan, reserving the chicken and discarding the vegetables. Add the rice to the stock, bring to the boil, then reduce the heat and simmer for 15 minutes, or until tender. Tear the chicken into shreds.

3 Whisk the egg whites until stiff peaks form, then beat in the yolks. Slowly beat in the lemon juice. Gently stir in 150 ml (5 fl oz) of the hot (not boiling) soup and beat thoroughly. Add the egg mixture to the soup and stir gently over low heat until thickened slightly. It should still be quite thin. Do not let it boil or the eggs may scramble. Add the shredded chicken, and season.

4 Set aside for 3–4 minutes to allow the flavours to develop, then sprinkle with the parsley. Garnish with the lemon slices and serve immediately.

INGREDIENTS

Chicken balls
500 g (1 lb 2 oz) minced (ground) chicken
1 small red chilli, finely chopped
2 garlic cloves, finely chopped
1/2 small red onion, finely chopped
1 stem lemon grass (white part only), finely chopped
2 tablespoons chopped coriander (cilantro) leaves

200 g (7 oz) dried rice vermicelli
1 tablespoon peanut oil
75 g (1/4 cup) good-quality laksa paste
1 litre (4 cups) chicken stock
500 ml (2 cups) coconut milk
8 fried tofu puffs, cut in half on the diagonal
90 g (1 cup) bean sprouts
2 tablespoons shredded Vietnamese mint
3 tablespoons shredded coriander (cilantro) leaves
lime wedges, to serve
fish sauce, to serve (optional)

1 To make the balls, process all the ingredients in a food processor until just combined. Roll tablespoons of mixture into balls with wet hands.

2 Place the vermicelli in a heatproof bowl, cover with boiling water and soak for 6–7 minutes. Drain well.

3 Heat the oil in a large saucepan over medium heat. Add the laksa paste and cook for 1–2 minutes, or until aromatic. Add the stock, reduce the heat and simmer for 10 minutes. Add the coconut milk and the chicken balls and simmer for 5 minutes, or until the balls are cooked through.

4 Divide the vermicelli, tofu puffs and bean sprouts among four serving bowls and ladle the soup over the top, dividing the balls evenly. Garnish with the mint and coriander leaves. Serve with the lime wedges and, if desired, fish sauce.

INGREDIENTS

200 g (1 cup) dried borlotti beans
50 g (1³/₄ oz) lard or butter
1 large onion, finely chopped
1 garlic clove, finely chopped
15 g (³/₄ cup) parsley, finely chopped
2 sage leaves
100 g (3¹/₂ oz) pancetta or bacon, cubed
2 celery stalks, halved then sliced
2 carrots, sliced
3 potatoes, peeled but left whole
1 teaspoon tomato paste (purée)
400 g (14 oz) can chopped tomatoes
8 basil leaves
3 litres (12 cups) chicken or vegetable stock
2 zucchini (courgettes), sliced
210 g (1¹/₃ cups) shelled peas
115 g (4 oz) runner beans, cut into 4 cm (1¹/₂ inch) lengths
¹/₄ cabbage, shredded
150 g (5¹/₂ oz) ditalini, avemarie or other small pasta
grated Parmesan cheese, to serve

Pesto
2 garlic cloves, crushed
50 g (¹/₃ cup) pine nuts
80 g (1³/₄ cups) firmly packed basil leaves
4 tablespoons grated Parmesan cheese
150 ml (5 fl oz) extra virgin olive oil

1 Put the dried borlotti beans in a large bowl, cover with cold water and leave to soak overnight. Drain and rinse under cold water.

2 Melt the lard in a large saucepan and add the onion, garlic, parsley, sage and pancetta. Cook over low heat, stirring once or twice, for 10 minutes, or until the onion is soft and golden.

3 Add the celery, carrot and potatoes and cook for 5 minutes. Stir in the tomato paste, tomato, basil and dried beans. Season with plenty of pepper. Add the stock and bring slowly to the boil. Cover and leave to simmer for 2 hours, stirring once or twice.

4 If the potatoes haven't already broken up, roughly break them up with a fork against the side of the pan. Taste for seasoning and add the zucchini, peas, runner beans, cabbage and pasta. Simmer until the pasta is al dente.

5 Meanwhile, to make the pesto, place the garlic, pine nuts, basil and Parmesan in a food processor and mix to a paste. Alternatively, use a mortar and pestle. Add the oil in a steady stream, mixing continuously. Season to taste. Serve the soup with a dollop of pesto and the Parmesan.

INGREDIENTS

300 g (10$\frac{1}{2}$ oz) minced (ground) pork
4 spring onions (scallions), sliced
3 garlic cloves, roughly chopped
2 teaspoons grated ginger
2 teaspoons cornflour (cornstarch)
125 ml ($\frac{1}{2}$ cup/4$\frac{1}{4}$ fl oz) light soy sauce
3 tablespoons Chinese rice wine
30 won ton wrappers
3 litres (12 cups/5$\frac{1}{2}$ pints) ready-made Chinese chicken broth, or home-made or ready-made chicken stock
200 g (7 oz) dried flat egg noodles
2 spring onions (scallions), extra, sliced on the diagonal
1 teaspoon sesame oil

1 Put the minced pork, spring onion, garlic, grated ginger, cornflour, 1$\frac{1}{2}$ tablespoons of the soy sauce and 1 tablespoon of the rice wine in a food processor and process until well combined. Place 2 teaspoons of the mixture in the centre of a won ton wrapper and lightly brush the edges with water. Lift the sides up tightly and pinch around the filling to form a pouch. Repeat this process to make 30 won tons.

2 Place the chicken broth in a large saucepan and bring to a simmer over medium–high heat. Stir in the remaining soy sauce and rice wine.

3 Meanwhile, bring a large pan of water to the boil. Reduce the heat, add the won tons and simmer for 1 minute, or until they float to the surface and are cooked through, then remove with a slotted spoon. Return the water to the boil, add the egg noodles and cook for 3 minutes, or until tender. Drain and add to the chicken broth along with the cooked won tons. Simmer for 2 minutes, or until heated through.

4 Divide the broth, noodles and won tons among six large serving bowls, sprinkle with extra spring onion and drizzle each with a little sesame oil.

LONG AND SHORT NOODLE SOUP

PRAWN LAKSA

INGREDIENTS

1 kg (2 lb) raw medium prawns (shrimp)
⅓ cup (80 ml/2¾ fl oz) oil
2–6 small fresh red chillies, seeded
1 onion, roughly chopped
3 cloves garlic, halved
2 cm x 2 cm (¾ inch x ¾ inch) piece fresh ginger or galangal, chopped
3 stems lemon grass (white part only), chopped
1 teaspoon ground turmeric
1 tablespoon ground coriander (cilantro)
2 teaspoons shrimp paste
2½ cups (625 ml/20 fl oz) coconut cream
2 teaspoons grated palm sugar or soft brown sugar
4 fresh kaffir lime (makrut) leaves, crushed
1–2 tablespoons fish sauce
200 g (6½ oz) packet fish balls
190 g (6½ oz) packet fried tofu puffs
250 g (8 oz) dried rice vermicelli
125 g (4 oz) bean sprouts
⅓ cup (20 g/¾ oz) chopped fresh mint
2 teaspoons fresh coriander (cilantro) leaves

1 Peel the prawns and gently pull out the dark vein from each prawn back, starting at the head end. Reserve the heads, shells and tails. Cover and refrigerate the prawn meat.

2 Heat 2 tablespoons of the oil in a wok or large saucepan and add the prawn shells and heads. Stir over medium heat for 10 minutes, or until orange, then add 1 litre water. Bring to the boil, then reduce the heat and simmer for 15 minutes. Strain the stock through a fine sieve, discarding the shells. Clean the pan.

3 Finely chop the chillies (use 2 for mild flavour, increase for hot), onion, garlic, ginger and lemon grass with the turmeric, coriander and ¼ cup (60 ml/2 fl oz) of the prawn stock in a food processor.

4 Heat the remaining oil in the pan, add the chilli mixture and shrimp paste, and stir over medium heat for 3 minutes, or until fragrant. Pour in the remaining stock and simmer for 10 minutes. Add the coconut cream, sugar, lime leaves and fish sauce, and simmer for 5 minutes. Add the prawns and simmer for 2 minutes, or until firm and light pink. Add the fish balls and tofu puffs, and simmer gently until just heated through.

5 Soak the rice vermicelli in a bowl of boiling water for 2 minutes, then drain and divide it among serving bowls. Top with the bean sprouts and ladle the soup over the top. Sprinkle with the mint and coriander.

INGREDIENTS

2 kg (4 lb 8 oz) oxtails, trimmed

2 tablespoons vegetable oil

2 onions, finely chopped

1 leek, finely chopped

2 carrots, diced

1 celery stalk, diced

2 garlic cloves, crushed

2 bay leaves

2 tablespoons tomato paste (purée)

1 thyme sprig

2 flat-leaf (Italian) parsley sprigs

3.5 litres (14 cups) chicken stock

375 ml (1½ cups) stout

2 tomatoes, seeded and diced

100 g (3½ oz) cauliflower florets

100 g (3½ oz) green beans

100 g (3½ oz) broccoli florets

100 g (3½ oz) asparagus, cut into 3 cm (1¼ inch) lengths

1   Preheat the oven to 200°C (400°F/Gas 6). Place the oxtails in a baking dish and bake for 1 hour, turning occasionally, or until dark golden. Leave to cool.

2   Heat the oil in a large saucepan over medium heat and cook the onion, leek, carrot and celery for 3–4 minutes, or until soft. Stir in the garlic, bay leaves and tomato paste, then add the oxtails, thyme and parsley.

3   Add the stock and bring to the boil over high heat. Reduce the heat and simmer for 3 hours, or until the oxtails are tender and the meat falls off the bone. Skim off any scum that rises to the surface. Remove the oxtails and cool slightly.

4   Take the meat off the bones and discard any fat or sinew. Roughly chop and add to the soup with the stout, tomato and 500 ml (2 cups/17 fl oz) water. Add the vegetables and simmer for 5 minutes, or until the vegetables are tender. Season.

SPICY PRAWNS

1 kg (2 lb) raw medium prawns (shrimp), peeled and
   deveined, tails intact (reserve shells and heads)
1 teaspoon ground turmeric
¼ cup (60 ml/2 fl oz) oil
2 onions, finely chopped
4–6 cloves garlic, finely chopped
1–2 small fresh green chillies, seeded and chopped
2 teaspoons ground cumin
2 teaspoons ground coriander (cilantro)
1 teaspoon paprika
⅓ cup (90 g/3 oz) plain yoghurt
⅓ cup (80 ml/2¾ fl oz) thick cream
⅓ cup (20 g/¾ oz) chopped fresh coriander (cilantro) leaves

1 Bring 1 litre water to the boil in a large saucepan. Add the reserved prawn shells and heads, reduce the heat and simmer for 2 minutes. Skim any scum that forms on the surface during cooking with a skimmer or slotted spoon. Drain, discard the shells and heads, and return the liquid to the pan. You will need 3 cups (750 ml/24 fl oz) liquid. Make up with water, if necessary. Add the turmeric and peeled prawns, and cook for 1 minute, or until the prawns just turn pink. Remove the prawns and set the stock aside.

2 Heat the oil in a large saucepan. Cook the onion, stirring, for 8 minutes, or until light golden brown. Take care not to burn the onion. Add the garlic and chilli, cook for 2 minutes, then add the cumin, coriander and paprika, and cook, stirring, for 2–3 minutes, or until fragrant.

3 Gradually add the reserved prawn stock, bring to the boil and cook, stirring occasionally, for 35 minutes, or until the mixture has reduced by half and thickened.

4 Remove from the heat and stir in the yoghurt. Add the prawns and stir over low heat for 2–3 minutes, or until the prawns are warmed through, but do now allow the mixture to boil. Stir in the cream and coriander leaves. Cover and leave to stand for 15 minutes to allow the flavours to infuse. Reheat gently and serve with rice.

INGREDIENTS

2 tablespoons oil
750 g (1½ lb) blade steak, thinly sliced
4 tablespoons Musaman curry paste
2 cloves garlic, finely chopped
1 onion, sliced lengthways
6 curry leaves, torn
3 cups (750 ml/24 fl oz) coconut milk
3 cups (450 g/14 oz) butternut pumpkin (squash), roughly diced
2 tablespoons chopped unsalted peanuts
1 tablespoon palm sugar
2 tablespoons tamarind purée
2 tablespoons fish sauce
curry leaves, to garnish

1 Heat a large wok or frying pan over high heat. Add the oil and swirl to coat the side. Add the meat in batches and cook for 5 minutes, or until browned. Remove the meat from the wok.

2 Add the Musaman curry paste, chopped garlic, onion and torn curry leaves to the wok, and stir to coat. Return the meat to the wok and cook, stirring, over medium heat for 2 minutes.

3 Add the coconut milk to the wok, then reduce the heat and simmer for 45 minutes. Add the diced pumpkin and simmer for 25–30 minutes, or until the meat and the vegetables are tender and the sauce has thickened.

4 Stir in the peanuts, palm sugar, tamarind purée and fish sauce, and simmer for 1 minute. Garnish with curry leaves. Serve with pickled vegetables and rice.

INGREDIENTS

1 kg (2 lb 4 oz) asparagus
500 ml (2 cups) chicken stock
500 ml (2 cups) vegetable stock
4 tablespoons olive oil
1 small onion, finely chopped
360 g (1²/₃ cups) risotto rice (arborio, vialone nano or carnaroli)
70 g (2¹/₂ oz) Parmesan cheese, grated
3 tablespoons thick (double/heavy) cream

1   Wash the asparagus and remove the woody ends (hold each spear at both ends and bend it gently — it will snap at its natural breaking point). Separate the tender spear tips from the stems.

2   Cook the asparagus stems in boiling water for 8 minutes, or until very tender. Drain and place in a blender with the chicken and vegetable stocks. Blend for 1 minute, then put in a saucepan, bring to the boil and maintain at a low simmer.

3   Cook the asparagus tips in boiling water for 1 minute, drain and refresh in iced water.

4   Heat the oil in a large wide heavy-based saucepan. Add the onion and cook until soft but not browned. Stir in the rice, season, and reduce the heat to low. Stir in a ladleful of the stock and cook over moderate heat, stirring continuously. When the stock has been absorbed, stir in another ladleful. Continue like this for about 20 minutes, until all the stock has been added and the rice is al dente. (You may not use all the stock, or you may need a little extra — every risotto will be slightly different.) Add the Parmesan and cream and gently stir in the asparagus tips. Season.

INGREDIENTS

2 tablespoons oil
1 teaspoon black mustard seeds
10 curry leaves
$^1/_4$ teaspoon ground turmeric
1 cm ($^1/_2$ inch) piece of ginger, grated
2 green chillies, finely chopped
2 onions, chopped
500 g (1 lb 2 oz) waxy potatoes, cut into 2 cm ($^3/_4$ inch) cubes
1 tablespoon tamarind purée

1 Heat the oil in a heavy-based frying pan, add the mustard seeds, cover, and when they start to pop add the curry leaves, turmeric, ginger, chilli and onion and cook, uncovered, until the onion is soft.

2 Add the potato cubes and 250 ml (1 cup/8$^1/_2$ fl oz) water to the pan, bring to the boil, cover and cook until the potato is tender and almost breaking up. If there is any liquid left in the pan, let it simmer a little, uncovered, until it evaporates. If the potato isn't cooked and there is no liquid left, add a little more and continue to cook. Add the tamarind and season with salt.

NOTE This filling is traditionally rolled in dosas — large pancakes made with rice flour — and served for breakfast or as a snack in southern India. However, it also makes an excellent spicy potato side dish.

LAMB HOTPOT

2 tablespoons olive oil

8 lamb shanks

2 onions, sliced

4 cloves garlic, finely chopped

3 bay leaves, torn in half

1–2 teaspoons hot paprika

2 teaspoons sweet paprika

1 tablespoon plain (all-purpose) flour

¼ cup (60 g/2 oz) tomato paste (purée)

1.5 (6½ cups) litres vegetable stock

4 potatoes, chopped

4 carrots, sliced

3 celery sticks, thickly sliced

3 tomatoes, seeded and chopped

1   To make the lamb stock, heat 1 tablespoon of the oil in a large, heavy-based saucepan over medium heat. Brown the shanks well in two batches, then drain on paper towels.

2   Add the remaining oil to the pan and cook the onion, garlic and bay leaves over low heat for 10 minutes, stirring regularly. Add the paprikas and flour and cook, stirring, for 2 minutes. Gradually add the combined tomato paste and vegetable stock. Bring to the boil, stirring continuously, and return the shanks to the pan. Reduce the heat to low and simmer, covered, for 1½ hours, stirring occasionally.

3   Remove and discard the bay leaves. Remove the shanks, allow to cool slightly and then cut the meat from the bone. Discard the bone. Cut the meat into pieces and refrigerate. Refrigerate the stock for about 1 hour, or until fat forms on the surface and can be spooned off.

4   Return the meat to the stock along with the potato, carrot and celery, and bring to the boil. Reduce the heat and simmer for 15 minutes. Season, and add the chopped tomato to serve.

500 g (1 lb 2 oz) Italian pork sausages

200 g (7 oz) piece speck (see note)

1 tablespoon olive oil

1 large onion, chopped

3 garlic cloves, crushed

1 celery stalk, cut in half and sliced

1 large carrot, cut into 1 cm ($^1/_2$ inch) cubes

bouquet garni (1 parsley sprig, 1 oregano sprig, 2 bay leaves)

1 small red chilli, halved lengthways

400 g (14 oz) can chopped tomatoes

1.75 litres (7 cups) chicken stock

300 g (10$^1/_2$ oz) Brussels sprouts, cut in half from top to base

300 g (10$^1/_2$ oz) green beans, cut into 3 cm (1$^1/_4$ inch) lengths

300 g (10$^1/_2$ oz) shelled broad beans, fresh or frozen

2 tablespoons chopped flat-leaf (Italian) parsley

1 Grill (broil) the sausages under a hot grill (broiler) for 8–10 minutes, turning occasionally, or until brown. Remove and cut into 3 cm (1$^1/_4$ inch) lengths. Trim and reserve the fat from the speck, then dice the speck.

2 Heat the oil in a large saucepan over medium heat. Add the speck and reserved speck fat and cook for 2–3 minutes, or until golden. Add the onion, garlic, celery and carrot, reduce the heat to low and cook for 6–8 minutes, or until softened. Discard the remains of the speck fat.

3 Stir in the sausages, bouquet garni, chilli and chopped tomato and cook for 5 minutes. Add the stock, bring to the boil, then reduce the heat and simmer for 1 hour. Add the Brussels sprouts, green beans and broad beans and simmer for 30 minutes. Discard the bouquet garni, then stir in the parsley. Season to taste. Divide among four bowls and serve.

NOTE Speck is cured smoked ham or pork belly. It has a strong taste and is usually cut into small pieces and used as a flavour base.

GRILLED ITALIAN SAUSAGE AND VEGETABLE SOUP

INGREDIENTS

500 g (1 lb) Shanghai noodles
700 g (1 lb 5 oz) boneless pork belly
2 teaspoons peanut oil
150 g (5 oz) caster sugar
5 cloves garlic, crushed
5 slices fresh ginger, 5 mm (¼ inch) thick
2 stems lemon grass (white part only), bruised
1 teaspoon ground white pepper
2 cups (500 ml/16 fl oz) chicken stock
3½ tablespoons fish sauce
100 g (3½ oz) canned bamboo shoots, well drained
4 spring onions, cut into 3 cm (1¼ inch) pieces
1 tablespoon lime juice
1 tablespoon chopped fresh coriander (cilantro) leaves

1   Cook the Shanghai noodles in a large saucepan of boiling water for 4–5 minutes, or until tender. Rinse, drain and cut into 10 cm lengths.

2   Preheat the oven to moderate 180°C (350°F/Gas 4). Cut the pork belly across the grain into 1 cm thick slices then cut each slice into 2 cm (³/₄ inch) pieces. Heat the oil in a 4 litre clay pot or flameproof casserole dish over medium–high heat. Cook the pork in two batches for about 5 minutes, or until it starts to brown all over. Remove the pork and drain the fat.

3   Add the sugar and 2 tablespoons water to the casserole dish, stirring until the sugar has dissolved and scraping up any sediment that may have stuck to the bottom. Increase the heat to high and cook for 2–3 minutes without stirring until dark golden, being careful not to burn—you should just be able to smell the caramel.

4   Return the pork to the casserole dish, then add the garlic, ginger, lemon grass, white pepper, stock, 2 tablespoons of the fish sauce and 1½ cups (375 ml/12 fl oz) water and stir to combine. Bake, covered, for 1 hour then remove the lid and cook for another hour, or until the pork is very tender. Carefully remove the ginger slices and the lemon grass.

5   Add the noodles to the casserole dish with the bamboo shoots, spring onion, lime juice and remaining fish sauce and stir to combine. Return the dish to the oven for 10 minutes to heat through. Stir in the chopped coriander, if desired, and serve immediately with steamed Asian greens.

600 g (1¼ lb) orange sweet potato (kumera)
2 tablespoons olive oil
1.5 kg (3 lb) chicken pieces
1 leek, cut into 2 cm (¾ inch) slices
2 cloves garlic, crushed
2 tablespoons plain (all-purpose) flour
2 cups (500 ml/16 fl oz) chicken stock
2 tablespoons fresh thyme

1 Preheat the oven to hot 220°C (425°F/Gas 7). Peel the sweet potato and cut it into chunks. Heat 1 tablespoon of the oil in a large flameproof casserole dish. Cook the chicken in batches for 3–4 minutes, or until browned. Set aside. Add the remaining oil and cook the leek and garlic for 2 minutes, or until soft.

2 Add the flour to the dish and cook, stirring, for about 1 minute to brown the flour. Gradually add the stock, stirring until the sauce boils and thickens. Remove from the heat. Return the chicken to the pan.

3 Add the sweet potato and half the thyme. Bake, covered, for 1½ hours, or until the chicken is cooked through and the sweet potato is tender. Season, and scatter with the remaining thyme. Serve with steamed rice.

INGREDIENTS

2 corn cobs (700 g/1 lb 9 oz)

1 tablespoon olive oil

1 red onion, finely chopped

1 small red chilli, finely chopped

$1/2$ teaspoon ground allspice

4 vine-ripened tomatoes, peeled and finely diced

1.5 litres (6 cups) fish stock or light chicken stock

300 g ($10^1/2$ oz) boneless firm white fish fillets (ling or perch), diced

200 g (7 oz) fresh crab meat

200 g (7 oz) peeled raw prawns (shrimp), roughly chopped

1 tablespoon lime juice

Quesadillas

4 flour tortillas (19 cm/$7^1/2$ inch)

85 g ($2/3$ cup) grated Cheddar cheese

4 tablespoons coriander (cilantro) leaves

2 tablespoons olive oil

1 Preheat the oven to 200°C (400°F/Gas 6). Peel back the husks on the corn cobs (making sure they stay intact at the base) and remove the silks. Fold the husks back over the corn, place in a baking dish and bake for 1 hour, or until the corn is tender.

2 Heat the oil in a large saucepan over medium heat. Add the onion and cook until soft. Add the chilli and allspice and cook for 1 minute, then add the tomato and stock and bring to the boil. Reduce the heat and simmer, covered, for 45 minutes.

3 Slice off the kernels from the corn cobs with a sharp knife, add to the soup and simmer, uncovered, for 15 minutes. Add the fish, crab and prawn meat to the soup and simmer for 5 minutes, or until the seafood is cooked. Stir in the lime juice and serve with the quesadillas, if desired.

4 To make the quesadillas, top one tortilla with half the cheese and half the coriander. Season, then top with another tortilla. Heat 1 tablespoon of the oil in a frying pan and cook the quesadilla for 30 seconds on each side, or until the cheese just begins to melt. Repeat to make the other quesadilla. Cut into wedges.

INGREDIENTS

165 g (³/₄ cup) dried chickpeas
1 tablespoon olive oil
850 g (1 lb 14 oz) boned lamb leg, cut into 1 cm (¹/₂ inch) cubes
1 onion, chopped
2 garlic cloves, crushed
¹/₂ teaspoon ground cinnamon
¹/₂ teaspoon ground turmeric
¹/₂ teaspoon ground ginger
4 tablespoons chopped coriander (cilantro) leaves
2 x 400 g (14 oz) cans chopped tomatoes
1 litre (4 cups) chicken stock
160 g (²/₃ cup) dried red lentils, rinsed
coriander (cilantro) leaves, to garnish

1 Soak the chickpeas in cold water overnight. Drain and rinse well.

2 Heat the oil in a large saucepan over high heat and brown the lamb in batches for 2–3 minutes. Reduce the heat to medium, return the lamb to the pan with the onion and garlic and cook for 5 minutes. Add the spices, season and cook for 2 minutes. Add the coriander, tomato, stock and 500 ml (2 cups) water and bring to the boil over high heat.

3 Add the lentils and chickpeas and simmer, covered, over low heat for 1¹/₂ hours. Uncover and cook for 30 minutes, or until the lamb is tender and the soup is thick. Season. Garnish with coriander.

LAMB SHANKS IN TOMATO SAUCE ON POLENTA

2 tablespoons olive oil

1 large red onion, sliced

4 French-trimmed lamb shanks (about 250 g/8 oz each)

2 cloves garlic, crushed

400 g (13 oz) can peeled, chopped tomatoes

½ cup (125 ml/4 fl oz) red wine

2 teaspoons chopped fresh rosemary

1 cup (150 g/5 oz) instant polenta

50 g (1¾ oz) butter

½ cup (50 g/1¾ oz) grated fresh Parmesan

1 Preheat the oven to warm 160°C (315°F/Gas 2–3). Heat the oil in a 4 litre flameproof casserole dish over medium heat and sauté the onion for 3–4 minutes, or until softening and becoming transparent. Add the lamb shanks and cook for 2–3 minutes, or until lightly browned. Add the garlic, tomato and wine, then bring to the boil and cook for 3–4 minutes. Stir in the rosemary. Season with ¼ teaspoon each of salt and pepper.

2 Cover and bake for 2 hours. Remove the lid, return to the oven and simmer for a further 15 minutes, or until the lamb just starts to fall off the bone. Check periodically that the sauce is not too dry, adding water if needed.

3 About 20 minutes before serving, bring 1 litre (4 cups) water to the boil in a saucepan. Add the polenta in a thin stream, whisking continuously, then reduce the heat to very low. Simmer for 8–10 minutes, or until thick and coming away from the side of the pan. Stir in the butter and Parmesan. To serve, spoon the polenta onto serving plates, top with the shanks and tomato sauce.

INGREDIENTS

1 leek, green part only
1 bay leaf
1 sprig fresh thyme
1 sprig celery leaves
4 sprigs fresh parsley
2 tablespoons butter
1 tablespoon oil
1 kg (2 lb) chuck or stewing steak, cubed
2 onions, sliced
2 cloves garlic, crushed
2 tablespoons plain flour
1½ cups (375 ml/12 fl oz) brown ale or stout
1 long bread stick
2 teaspoons French mustard
2 teaspoons butter, softened

1   To make a bouquet garni, wrap the green part of the leek around the bay leaf, thyme sprig, celery leaves and parsley, then tie with string. Leave a long tail to the string for easy removal.

2   Preheat the oven to moderate 180°C (350°F/Gas 4). Heat the butter and oil in a large pan and cook the beef in batches for 3–4 minutes, or until well browned. Remove from the pan. Lower the heat and cook the onion and garlic for 4 minutes, or until translucent. Sprinkle in the flour, stir well, then cook for 1 minute. Combine the beer with 1½ cups (375 ml/12 fl oz) water and add the pan. Stir well, scraping the pan to incorporate ingredients that are stuck to the base. Bring to the boil and return the meat to the pan. Add the bouquet garni and return to the boil. Transfer to a 2.5 litre (10 cup) casserole dish, cover well with foil and cook gently in the oven for 2½ hours.

3   Cut the bread into 2 cm (¾ inch) slices and spread with the combined mustard and butter. Remove the casserole from the oven, take out the bouquet garni and skim off any fat. Put the bread slices on the surface of the casserole, mustard-side-up, and press down gently to cover with juice. Return to the oven and cook, uncovered, for another 30–40 minutes, or until the bread becomes crusty. Serve with steamed green vegetables.

LION'S HEAD MEATBALLS

INGREDIENTS

Chicken stock
1.5 kg (3 lb) chicken bones (chicken necks, backs, wings), washed
2 slices fresh ginger, cut into 1 cm (½ inch) thick slices
4 spring onions

6 dried Chinese mushrooms
100 g (3½ oz) mung bean vermicelli
600 g (1¼ lb) minced (ground) pork
1 egg white
4 cloves garlic, finely chopped
1 tablespoon finely grated fresh ginger
1 tablespoon cornflour (cornstarch)
1½ tablespoons Chinese rice wine
6 spring onions, thinly sliced
2 tablespoons peanut oil
¼ cup (60 ml/2 fl oz) light soy sauce
1 teaspoon sugar
400 g (13 oz) bok choy, halved lengthways, leaves separated

1 To make the stock, place the bones and 3.5 litres (15 cups) water in a large saucepan and bring to a simmer—do not let it boil. Remove the scum from the surface and continue doing so over the next 30 minutes. Add the ginger and spring onions, and cook, partially covered, keeping at a low simmer for 3 hours. Strain through a fine sieve. Cool. Cover and refrigerate overnight. Remove the layer of fat from the surface once it has solidified.

2 Soak the Chinese mushrooms in 1 cup (250 ml/8 fl oz) boiling water for 20 minutes. Drain. Discard the stems and thinly slice the caps. Meanwhile, place the vermicelli in a heatproof bowl, cover with boiling water and soak for 3–4 minutes, or until soft. Drain and rinse. Preheat the oven to hot 220°C (425°F/Gas 7).

3 Place the mince, egg white, garlic, ginger, cornflour, rice wine, two-thirds of the spring onion and salt, to taste, in a food processor. Using the pulse button, process until smooth and well combined. Divide the mixture into eight portions and shape into large balls with wet hands.

4 Place 2 cups (500 ml/16 fl oz) of the stock (freeze any remaining stock) in a large saucepan and bring to the boil over high heat, then remove from the heat and keep warm.

5 Heat the oil in a wok over high heat. Fry the meatballs in batches for 2 minutes each side, or until golden, but not cooked through. Drain.

6 Place the meatballs, mushrooms, soy sauce and sugar in a 2.5 litre (10 cup) ovenproof clay pot or casserole dish, and cover with the hot stock. Bake, covered, for 45 minutes. Add the bok choy and noodles and bake, covered, for another 10 minutes. Sprinkle with the remaining spring onion, and serve.

30 g (1 oz) butter
125 g (4 oz) bacon, roughly chopped
1.5 kg (3 lb) skinless chicken pieces
350 g (11 oz) baby onions
2 tablespoons plain (all-purpose) flour
3 cups (750 ml/24 fl oz) red wine
250 g (8 oz) mushrooms, sliced
1 tablespoon fresh thyme leaves, to garnish

1 Preheat the oven to moderate 180°C (350°F/Gas 4). Melt the butter in a large flameproof casserole dish over medium heat. Add the bacon and cook until golden, then remove. Add the chicken pieces and cook, in batches, for 4–5 minutes, or until browned. Remove. Add the onions and cook for 2–3 minutes, or until browned, then remove from the dish.

2 Stir the flour in to the dish, then remove from the heat and slowly pour in the red wine, while stirring. Return to the heat, bring to the boil and return the bacon and chicken to the dish. Cover and bake for 1 hour. Return the onions to the dish and add the mushrooms. Cook for a further 30 minutes. Season to taste with salt and freshly ground black pepper, and garnish with the thyme. Serve with mashed potato, if desired.

CHICKEN AND RED WINE CASSEROLE

INGREDIENTS

1$^1/_2$ cups (300 g/10 oz) borlotti beans or red kidney beans
1 kg (2 lb) boned leg of lamb
1$^1/_2$ tablespoons olive oil
2 rashers bacon, rind removed, chopped
1 large onion, chopped
2 cloves garlic, crushed
1 large carrot, chopped
2 cups (500 ml/16 fl oz) dry red wine
1 tablespoon tomato paste (purée)
1$^1/_2$ cups (375 ml/12 fl oz) beef stock
2 large sprigs fresh rosemary
2 sprigs fresh thyme

1   Put the beans in a bowl and cover with plenty of water. Leave to soak overnight, then drain well.

2   Preheat the oven to warm 160°C (315°F/Gas 2–3). Trim any excess fat from the lamb and cut the lamb into 3 cm (1$^1/_4$ inch) pieces.

3   Heat 1 tablespoon of the oil in a large flameproof casserole dish. Add half the meat and toss over medium–high heat for 2 minutes, or until browned. Remove from the casserole and repeat with the remaining lamb. Remove from the casserole.

4   Heat the remaining olive oil in the casserole and add the bacon and onion. Cook over medium heat for 3 minutes, or until the onion is translucent. Add the garlic and carrot, and cook for 1 minute, or until the mixture is aromatic.

5   Return the meat and any juices to the casserole, increase the heat to high and add the wine. Bring to the boil and cook for 2 minutes. Add the beans, tomato paste, stock, rosemary and thyme, return to the boil, then cover and bake for 2 hours, or until the meat is tender. Stir occasionally during cooking. Skim off any excess fat, remove the sprigs of herbs, and season. Serve with bread.

INGREDIENTS

20 g (³/₄ oz) dried porcini mushrooms
1.5 kg (3 lb) chicken pieces
¹/₄ cup (30 g/1 oz) seasoned plain (all-purpose) flour
2 tablespoons oil
1 large onion, chopped
2 cloves garlic, crushed
¹/₄ cup (60 ml/2 fl oz) chicken stock
¹/₃ cup (80 ml/2³/₄ fl oz) white wine
425 g (14 oz) can peeled whole tomatoes
1 tablespoon balsamic vinegar
3 sprigs fresh thyme
1 bay leaf
300 g (10 oz) field mushrooms, thickly sliced

1   Preheat the oven to moderate 180°C (350°F/Gas 4). Put the porcini mushrooms in a bowl and cover with ¹/₄ cup (60 ml/2 fl oz) boiling water. Leave for 5 minutes, or until the mushrooms are rehydrated.

2   Lightly toss the chicken in the seasoned flour to coat, and shake off any excess.

3   Heat the oil in a flameproof casserole dish, and cook the chicken over medium heat in batches until well browned all over. Set aside. Add the onion and garlic to the casserole, and cook for 3–5 minutes, or until the onion softens. Stir in the chicken stock.

4   Return the chicken to the casserole with the porcini mushrooms (and any remaining liquid), wine, tomatoes, vinegar, thyme and bay leaf. Cover and bake for 30 minutes.

5   After 30 minutes, remove the lid and add the field mushrooms. Return to the oven and cook, uncovered, for 15–20 minutes, or until the sauce thickens slightly. Serve immediately.

WINTER LAMB SHANK SOUP

1 tablespoon olive oil
1.25 kg (2 lb 12 oz) lamb shanks
2 onions, chopped
4 garlic cloves, chopped
250 ml (1 cup) red wine
2 bay leaves
1 tablespoon chopped rosemary
2.5 litres (10 cups) beef stock
425 g (15 oz) can crushed tomatoes
165 g ($^3/_4$ cup) pearl barley, rinsed and drained
1 large carrot, diced
1 potato, diced
1 turnip, diced
1 parsnip, diced
2 tablespoons redcurrant jelly (optional)

1 Heat the oil in a large saucepan over high heat. Cook the lamb shanks for 2–3 minutes, or until brown. Remove.

2 Add the onion to the pan and cook over low heat for 8 minutes, or until soft. Add the garlic and cook for 30 seconds, then add the wine and simmer for 5 minutes.

3 Add the shanks, bay leaves, half the rosemary and 1.5 litres (6 cups) of the stock to the pan. Season. Bring to the boil over high heat. Reduce the heat and simmer, covered, for 2 hours, or until the meat falls off the bone. Remove the shanks and cool slightly.

4 Take the meat off the bone and roughly chop. Add to the broth with the tomato, barley, the remaining rosemary and stock and simmer for 30 minutes. Add the vegetables and cook for 1 hour, or until the barley is tender. Remove the bay leaves, then stir in the redcurrant jelly.

INGREDIENTS

1/4 cup (60 ml/2 fl oz) oil
1 kg (2 lb) pork fillets, cut into bite-size pieces
2 onions, finely chopped
4 cloves garlic, finely chopped
1 tablespoon finely chopped fresh ginger
1 tablespoon garam masala
2 teaspoons brown mustard seeds
4 tablespoons vindaloo paste

1 Heat the oil in a saucepan, add the pork in small batches and cook over medium heat for 5–7 minutes, or until browned. Remove from the pan.

2 Add the onion, garlic, ginger, garam masala and mustard seeds to the pan, and cook, stirring, for 5 minutes, or until the onion is soft.

3 Return all the meat to the pan, add the vindaloo paste and cook, stirring, for 2 minutes. Add 2 1/2 cups (625 ml/21 fl oz) water and bring to the boil. Reduce the heat and simmer, covered, for 1 1/2 hours, or until the meat is tender. Serve with boiled rice and pappadums.

INGREDIENTS

2 tablespoons soy bean oil, or oil
500 g (1 lb) firm white fish (ling, perch), cut into 2 cm (¾ inch) cubes
250 g (8 oz) raw prawns (shrimp), peeled and deveined, tails intact
2 x 400 ml (13 fl oz) cans coconut milk
1 tablespoon red curry paste
4 fresh or 8 dried kaffir lime (makrut) leaves
2 tablespoons fish sauce
2 tablespoons finely chopped fresh lemon grass (white part only)
2 cloves garlic, crushed
1 tablespoon finely chopped fresh galangal
1 tablespoon shaved palm sugar or soft brown sugar
300 g (10 oz) silken firm tofu, cut into 1.5 cm (⅝ inch) cubes
½ cup (125 g/4 oz) bamboo shoots, julienned
1 large fresh red chilli, thinly sliced
2 teaspoons lime juice
spring onions, chopped, to garnish
fresh coriander (cilantro) leaves, chopped, to garnish

1   Heat the oil in a large frying pan or wok over medium heat. Sear the fish and prawns for 1 minute on each side. Remove the fish and prawns from the pan.

2   Place ¼ cup (60 ml/2 fl oz) of the coconut milk and the curry paste in the pan, and cook over medium heat for 2 minutes, or until fragrant and the oil separates. Add the remaining coconut milk, kaffir lime leaves, fish sauce, lemon grass, garlic, galangal, palm sugar and 1 teaspoon salt. Cook over low heat for 15 minutes.

3   Add the tofu cubes, bamboo shoots and sliced chilli. Simmer for a further 3–5 minutes. Return to medium heat, add the seafood and lime juice, and cook for a further 3 minutes, or until the seafood is just cooked. Remove from the heat.

4   Serve the curry with steamed rice and garnish with the spring onion and coriander leaves.

INGREDIENTS

1 tablespoon ghee or oil
2 onions, chopped
$1/2$ cup (125 g/4 oz) plain yoghurt
1 teaspoon chilli powder
1 tablespoon ground coriander (cilantro)
2 teaspoons ground cumin
1 teaspoon ground cardamom
$1/2$ teaspoon ground cloves
1 teaspoon ground turmeric
3 cloves garlic, crushed
1 tablespoon grated fresh ginger
400 g (13 oz) can chopped tomatoes
1 kg (2 lb) boned leg of lamb, cut into 2.5 cm (1 inch) cubes
$1/4$ cup (30 g/1 oz) slivered almonds
1 teaspoon garam masala
chopped fresh coriander (cilantro) leaves, to garnish

1 Heat the ghee in a large saucepan, add the onion and cook, stirring, for 5 minutes, or until soft. Stir in the yoghurt, chilli powder, coriander, cumin, cardamom, cloves, turmeric, garlic and ginger. Add the tomato and 1 teaspoon salt, and simmer for 5 minutes.

2 Add the lamb and stir until coated. Cover and cook over low heat, stirring occasionally, for $1-1\frac{1}{2}$ hours, or until the lamb is tender. Uncover and simmer until the liquid thickens.

3 Meanwhile, toast the almonds in a dry frying pan over medium heat for 3–4 minutes, shaking the pan gently, until the nuts are golden brown. Remove from the pan at once to prevent them burning.

4 Add the garam masala to the curry and mix through well. Sprinkle the slivered almonds and coriander leaves over the top, and serve.

INGREDIENTS

1 tablespoon peanut oil

8 spring onions, sliced on the diagonal into 3 cm (1$^{1}/_{4}$ inch) lengths

2 cloves garlic, crushed

2–4 tablespoons red curry paste

750 g (1$^{1}/_{4}$ lb) Chinese roast duck, chopped

400 ml (13 fl oz) can coconut milk

450 g (14 oz) can pineapple pieces in syrup, drained

3 kaffir lime (makrut) leaves

$^{1}/_{4}$ cup (15 g/$^{1}/_{2}$ oz) chopped fresh coriander (cilantro)

2 tablespoons chopped fresh mint

1   Heat a wok until very hot, add the peanut oil and swirl to coat the side. Add the spring onion, garlic and red curry paste, and stir-fry for 1 minute, or until fragrant.

2   Add the roast duck pieces, coconut milk, drained pineapple pieces, kaffir lime leaves, and half the fresh coriander and mint. Bring to the boil, then reduce the heat and simmer for 10 minutes, or until the duck is heated through and the sauce has thickened slightly. Stir in the remaining fresh coriander and mint, and serve with steamed jasmine rice.

INGREDIENTS

4 raw large blue swimmer or mud crabs
1 tablespoon oil
1 large onion, finely chopped
2 cloves garlic, crushed
1 stem lemon grass, white part only, finely chopped
1 teaspoon sambal oelek
1 teaspoon ground cumin
1 teaspoon ground turmeric
1 teaspoon ground coriander (cilantro)
270 ml (9 fl oz) light coconut cream
2 cups (500 ml/16 fl oz) chicken stock
⅓ cup (20 g/¾ oz) firmly packed fresh basil leaves

1 Pull back the apron and remove the top shell from the crabs. Remove the intestines and grey feathery gills. Cut each crab into four pieces. Use a cracker to crack the claws open; this will make it easier to eat later and will also allow the flavours to get into the crab meat.

2 Heat the oil in a large saucepan or wok. Add the onion, garlic, lemon grass and sambal oelek and cook for 2–3 minutes, or until softened.

3 Add the cumin, turmeric, coriander and ½ teaspoon salt, and cook for a further 2 minutes, or until fragrant.

4 Stir in the coconut cream and stock. Bring to the boil, then reduce the heat, add the crab pieces and cook, stirring occasionally, for 10 minutes, or until the liquid has reduced and thickened slightly and the crabs are cooked through. Stir in the basil and serve with steamed rice.

MADRAS BEEF CURRY

1 kg (2 lb) skirt or chuck steak
1 tablespoon oil
1 onion, chopped
3–4 tablespoons Madras curry paste
¼ cup (60 g/2 oz) tomato paste (purée)
1 cup (250 ml/8 fl oz) beef stock

1   Trim the meat of any fat or sinew and cut it into bite-sized cubes. Heat the oil in a large frying pan, add the onion and cook over medium heat for 10 minutes, or until browned.

2   Add the curry paste and stir for 1 minute, or until fragrant. Then add the meat and cook, stirring, until coated with the curry paste. Stir in the tomato paste and stock. Reduce the heat and simmer, covered, for 1 hour 15 minutes. Uncover and simmer for 15 minutes, or until the meat is tender.

INGREDIENTS

2 kg (4 lb) leg of lamb, boned
1 onion, chopped
2 teaspoons grated fresh ginger
3 cloves garlic
2 teaspoons ground coriander (cilantro)
2 teaspoons ground cumin
1 teaspoon cardamom seeds
large pinch cayenne pepper
2 tablespoons ghee or oil
1 onion, extra, sliced
2½ tablespoons tomato paste (purée)
½ cup (125 g/4 oz) plain yoghurt
½ cup (125 ml/4 fl oz) coconut cream
½ cup (95 g/3 oz) ground almonds
toasted slivered almonds, to serve

1 Trim any excess fat or sinew from the leg of lamb, then cut the meat into 3 cm (1¼ inch) cubes and place in a large bowl.

2 Place the onion, ginger, garlic, coriander, cumin, cardamom seeds, cayenne pepper and ½ teaspoon salt in a food processor, and process to a smooth paste. Add the spice mixture to the lamb and mix well to coat. Leave to marinate for 1 hour.

3 Heat the ghee in a large saucepan, add the extra sliced onion and cook, stirring, over low heat for 7 minutes, or until the onion is soft. Add the lamb mixture and cook, stirring constantly, for 8–10 minutes, or until the lamb changes colour. Stir in the tomato paste, yoghurt, coconut cream and ground almonds.

4 Reduce the heat and simmer, covered, stirring occasionally, for 50 minutes, or until the meat is tender. Add a little water if the mixture becomes too dry. Season with salt and pepper, and garnish with the slivered almonds. Serve with rice.

INGREDIENTS

1 kg (2 lb) chicken thigh fillets
⅓ cup (80 ml/2¾ fl oz) oil
1 large red onion, finely chopped
4–5 cloves garlic, finely chopped
1 tablespoon grated fresh ginger
2 teaspoons ground cumin
2 teaspoons ground coriander (cilantro)
1 teaspoon ground turmeric
½ teaspoon chilli powder
425 g (14 oz) can chopped tomatoes
1 green capsicum (pepper), seeded and diced
1–2 small green chillies, seeded and finely chopped
4 tablespoons chopped fresh coriander (cilantro)
2 chopped spring onions, to garnish

1 Remove any excess fat or sinew from the chicken thigh fillets and cut into four or five even-sized pieces.

2 Heat a large wok over high heat, add the oil and swirl to coat the side. Add the onion and stir-fry over medium heat for 5 minutes, or until softened but not browned. Add the garlic and ginger and stir-fry for 3 more minutes.

3 Add the spices, 1 teaspoon salt and ¼ cup (60 ml/2 fl oz) water. Increase the heat to high and stir-fry for 2 minutes, or until the mixture has thickened. Take care not to burn.

4 Add the tomato and 1 cup (250 ml/8 fl oz) water and cook, stirring often, for a further 10 minutes, or until the mixture is thick and pulpy and the oil comes to the surface.

5 Add the chicken to the pan, reduce the heat and simmer, stirring often, for 15 minutes. Add the capsicum and chilli and simmer for 25 minutes, or until the chicken is tender. Add a little water if the mixture is too thick. Stir in the coriander and garnish with the spring onion.

Curry paste

2 tomatoes, peeled, seeded and roughly chopped

5 small fresh red chillies, seeded and chopped

5 cloves garlic, chopped

2 stems lemon grass (white part only), sliced

1 tablespoon coriander (cilantro) seeds, dry-roasted and ground

1 teaspoon shrimp powder, dry-roasted (see note)

1 tablespoon ground almonds

1/4 teaspoon ground nutmeg

1 teaspoon ground turmeric

3 tablespoons tamarind purée

1 tablespoon lime juice

250 g (8 oz) swordfish, cut into 3 cm (1 1/4 inch) cubes

1/4 cup (60 ml/2 fl oz) oil

2 red onions, chopped

2 small fresh red chillies, seeded and sliced

400 g (13 oz) raw medium prawns (shrimp), peeled and deveined, tails intact

250 g (8 oz) calamari (squid) tubes, cut into 1 cm (1/2 inch) rings

1/2 cup (125 ml/4 fl oz) fish stock

fresh Thai basil leaves, shredded, to garnish

1 To make the curry paste, place all the ingredients in a blender or food processor, and blend to a thick paste.

2 Place the lime juice in a bowl and season with salt and freshly ground black pepper. Add the swordfish, toss to coat well and leave to marinate for 20 minutes.

3 Heat the oil in a saucepan or wok, add the onion, sliced red chilli and curry paste, and cook, stirring occasionally, over low heat for 10 minutes, or until fragrant.

4 Add the swordfish and prawns, and stir to coat in the curry paste mixture. Cook for 3 minutes, or until the prawns just turn pink, then add the calamari and cook for 1 minute.

5 Add the stock and bring to the boil, then reduce the heat and simmer for 2 minutes, or until the seafood is cooked and tender. Season to taste with salt and freshly ground black pepper. Garnish with the shredded fresh basil leaves.

BALINESE SEAFOOD CURRY

INGREDIENTS

Curry paste

2 red onions, chopped

4 small fresh red chillies, seeded and sliced

4 cloves garlic, sliced

2 stems lemon grass (white part only), sliced

3 cm x 2 cm (1$\frac{1}{4}$ inch x $\frac{3}{4}$ inch) piece fresh galangal, sliced

8 kaffir lime (makrut) leaves, roughly chopped

1 teaspoon ground turmeric

$\frac{1}{2}$ teaspoon shrimp paste, dry-roasted

2 tablespoons oil

750 g (1$\frac{1}{2}$ lb) chicken thigh fillets, cut into bite-size pieces

400 ml (13 fl oz) can coconut milk

3 tablespoons tamarind purée

1 tablespoon fish sauce

3 kaffir lime (makrut) leaves, shredded

1   To make the curry paste, place all the ingredients in a food processor or blender and process to a thick paste.

2   Heat a wok or large saucepan over high heat, add the oil and swirl to coat the side. Add the curry paste and cook, stirring occasionally, over low heat for 8–10 minutes, or until fragrant. Add the chicken and stir-fry with the paste for 2–3 minutes.

3   Add the coconut milk, tamarind purée and fish sauce to the wok, and simmer, stirring occasionally, for 15–20 minutes, or until the chicken is tender. Garnish with the lime leaves. Serve with rice and steamed bok choy.

2 x 270 ml (9 fl oz) cans coconut cream (do not shake the cans)

3 tablespoons chu chee curry paste

500 g (1 lb) scallops, with roe removed

500 g (1 lb) raw medium king prawns (shrimp), peeled and deveined, tails intact

2–3 tablespoons fish sauce

2–3 tablespoons palm sugar or soft brown sugar

8 kaffir lime (makrut) leaves, finely shredded

2 fresh red chillies, thinly sliced

1 cup (30 g/1 oz) fresh Thai basil leaves

1 Place 1 cup (250 ml/8 fl oz) of the thick coconut cream from the top of the can in a wok. Heat until just boiling, then stir in the curry paste, reduce the heat and simmer for 10 minutes, or until fragrant and the oil begins to separate.

2 Stir in the remaining coconut cream, scallops and prawns, and cook for 5 minutes, or until tender. Add the fish sauce, palm sugar, kaffir lime leaves and chilli, and cook for 1 minute. Stir in half the basil and garnish with the remaining leaves.

CHU CHEE SEAFOOD

INGREDIENTS

1 cup (250 ml/8 fl oz) coconut cream (do not shake the can)
2 tablespoons red curry paste
500 g (1 lb) round or topside steak, cut into strips (see note)
2 tablespoons fish sauce
1 tablespoon palm sugar or soft brown sugar
5 kaffir lime (makrut) leaves, halved
2 cups (500 ml/16 fl oz) coconut milk
8 Thai eggplants, halved
2 tablespoons finely shredded fresh Thai basil leaves

1 Place the thick coconut cream from the top of the can in a wok and bring to the boil. Boil for 10 minutes, or until the oil starts to separate. Add the curry paste and simmer, stirring to prevent it sticking to the bottom, for 5 minutes, or until fragrant.

2 Add the meat and cook, stirring, for 3–5 minutes, or until it changes colour. Add the fish sauce, palm sugar, lime leaves, coconut milk and remaining coconut cream, and simmer for 1 hour, or until the meat is tender and the sauce has slightly thickened.

3 Add the eggplant and cook for 10 minutes, or until tender. If the sauce is too thick, add a little water. Stir in half the shredded basil leaves. Garnish with the remaining basil leaves and serve with rice.

NOTE Cut the meat into 5 x 5 x 2 cm (2 x 2 x $^3/_4$ inch) pieces, then cut across the grain at a 45° angle into 5 mm ($^1/_4$ inch) thick slices.

2 garlic cloves, crushed

3 small green chillies, seeded and finely chopped

$1/2$ teaspoon ground turmeric

$1/2$ teaspoon ground cloves

$1/2$ teaspoon ground cinnamon

$1/2$ teaspoon ground cayenne pepper

1 tablespoon tamarind purée

170 ml ($2/3$ cup) oil

800 g (1 lb 12 oz) pomfret, sole or leatherjacket fillets, skinned

310 ml ($1 1/4$ cups) coconut cream

2 tablespoons chopped coriander (cilantro) leaves

1   Mix together the garlic, chilli, spices, tamarind and 125 ml ($1/2$ cup) of the oil. Place the fish fillets in a shallow dish and spoon the marinade over them. Turn the fish over, cover and refrigerate for 30 minutes.

2   Heat the remaining oil in a large heavy-based frying pan and add the fish in batches. Cook for 1 minute on each side. Return all the fish to the pan, then reduce the heat to low and add any remaining marinade and the coconut cream. Season with salt and gently cook for 3–5 minutes, or until the fish is cooked through and flakes easily. If the sauce is too runny, lift out the fish, simmer the sauce for a few minutes, then pour it over the fish. Garnish with the coriander leaves.

BOMBAY-STYLE FISH

INGREDIENTS

Curry paste

10–12 large dried red chillies
1 teaspoon white pepper
4 red Asian shallots, chopped
4 garlic cloves, sliced
1 stem lemon grass, white part only, sliced
1 tablespoon finely chopped galangal
2 small coriander (cilantro) roots, chopped
1 tablespoon finely chopped ginger
1 tablespoon shrimp paste, dry roasted

1 tablespoon peanut oil
1 garlic clove, crushed
1 tablespoon fish sauce
30 g ($^1/_4$ cup) ground candlenuts
310 ml ($1^1/_4$ cups) fish stock
1 tablespoon whisky
3 kaffir lime (makrut) leaves, torn
600 g (1 lb 5 oz) raw prawns (shrimp), peeled and deveined, with tails intact
1 small carrot, quartered lengthways and sliced thinly on the diagonal
150 g ($5^1/_2$ oz) snake beans (yard-long beans), cut into 2 cm ($^3/_4$ inch) lengths
50 g ($^1/_4$ cup) bamboo shoots
Thai basil leaves, to garnish

1   To make the curry paste, soak the chillies in boiling water for 15 minutes. Drain and chop. Place in a food processor with the white pepper, shallots, garlic, lemon grass, galangal, coriander roots, ginger, shrimp paste and 1 teaspoon salt and blend until smooth — add a little water, if necessary, to form a paste.

2   Heat a wok over medium heat, add the oil and swirl to coat the side. Add the garlic and 3 tablespoons of the curry paste and cook, stirring, for 5 minutes. Add the fish sauce, ground candlenuts, fish stock, whisky, lime leaves, prawns, carrot, beans and bamboo shoots. Bring to the boil, then reduce the heat and simmer for 5 minutes, or until the prawns and vegetables are cooked.

3   Garnish with Thai basil and freshly ground black pepper.

INGREDIENTS

Paste

8–10 large dried red chillies

6 red Asian shallots, chopped

6 garlic cloves, chopped

1 teaspoon ground coriander (cilantro)

1 tablespoon ground cumin

1 teaspoon white pepper

2 stems lemon grass, white part only, bruised and sliced

1 tablespoon chopped galangal

6 coriander (cilantro) roots

2 teaspoons shrimp paste

2 tablespoons roasted peanuts

1 tablespoon peanut oil

400 ml (14 fl oz) can coconut cream

1 kg (2 lb 4 oz) round or blade steak, cut into 1 cm (¹/₂ inch) slices

400 ml (14 fl oz) can coconut milk

90 g (¹/₃ cup) crunchy peanut butter

4 kaffir lime (makrut) leaves

3 tablespoons lime juice

2¹/₂ tablespoons fish sauce

3–4 tablespoons grated palm sugar or soft brown sugar

1 tablespoon chopped roasted peanuts, extra, to garnish

Thai basil, to garnish

1 To make the paste, soak the chillies in a bowl of boiling water for 15 minutes, or until soft. Remove the seeds and chop. Place in a food processor with the shallots, garlic, ground coriander, ground cumin, white pepper, lemon grass, galangal, coriander roots, shrimp paste and peanuts and process until smooth — add a little water if the paste is too thick.

2 Place the peanut oil and the thick coconut cream from the top of the can (reserve the rest) in a saucepan and cook over medium heat for 10 minutes, or until the oil separates. Add 6–8 tablespoons of the paste and cook, stirring, for 5–8 minutes, or until fragrant.

3 Add the beef, coconut milk, peanut butter, lime leaves and the reserved coconut cream. Cook for 8 minutes, or until the beef just starts to change colour. Reduce the heat and simmer for 1 hour, or until the beef is tender.

4 Stir in the lime juice, fish sauce and sugar. Serve garnished with the peanuts and Thai basil.

INGREDIENTS

18 dried apricots
1 tablespoon ghee or oil
2 x 1.5 kg (3 lb) chickens, jointed
3 onions, thinly sliced
1 teaspoon grated fresh ginger
3 cloves garlic, crushed
3 large fresh green chillies, seeded and finely chopped
1 teaspoon cumin seeds
1 teaspoon chilli powder
$^1/_2$ teaspoon ground turmeric
4 cardamom pods, bruised
4 large tomatoes, peeled and cut into eighths

1 Soak the dried apricots in 1 cup (250 ml/8 fl oz) hot water for 1 hour.

2 Melt the ghee in a large saucepan, add the chicken in batches and cook over high heat for 5–6 minutes, or until browned. Remove from the pan. Add the onion and cook, stirring often, for 10 minutes, or until the onion has softened and turned golden brown.

3 Add the ginger, garlic and chopped green chilli, and cook, stirring, for 2 minutes. Stir in the cumin seeds, chilli powder and ground turmeric, and cook for a further 1 minute.

4 Return the chicken to the pan, add the cardamom, tomato and apricots, with any remaining liquid, and mix well. Simmer, covered, for 35 minutes, or until the chicken is tender.

5 Remove the chicken, cover and keep warm. Bring the liquid to the boil and boil rapidly, uncovered, for 5 minutes, or until it has thickened slightly. To serve, spoon the liquid over the chicken. Serve with steamed rice mixed with raisins, grated carrot and toasted flaked almonds.

INGREDIENTS

Spice paste

2 onions, chopped

2 cloves garlic, chopped

2 teaspoons grated lemon rind

2 small fresh red chillies, chopped

2 teaspoons ground coriander (cilantro)

2 teaspoons ground cumin

1 teaspoon ground turmeric

$1/2$ teaspoon ground cardamom

1 teaspoon garam masala

2 tablespoons oil

1 kg (2 lb) lean chuck steak, cut into 3 cm ($1^1/_4$ inch) cubes

$3/_4$ cup (185 ml/6 fl oz) coconut cream

1 tablespoon tamarind sauce

500 g (1 lb) baby potatoes, halved

1 To make the spice paste, combine all the ingredients in a food processor or blender, and process for 1 minute, or until very finely chopped.

2 Heat the oil in a heavy-based saucepan. Cook the meat quickly in small batches over medium–high heat until well browned. Drain on paper towels.

3 Add the spice paste to the pan and stir over medium heat for 2 minutes. Return the meat to the pan with the coconut cream, tamarind sauce and $1/2$ cup (125 ml/4 fl oz) water, and bring to the boil. Reduce the heat to a simmer and cook, covered, for 30 minutes, stirring occasionally.

4 Add the potato and cook, covered, for 30 minutes. Remove the lid and cook for 30 minutes, or until the meat is tender and almost all of the liquid has evaporated.

PORK AND CORIANDER STEW

1½ tablespoons coriander (cilantro) seeds
800 g (1 lb 10 oz) pork fillet, cubed
1 tablespoon plain (all-purpose) flour
2 tablespoons olive oil
1 large onion, thinly sliced
1½ cups (375 ml/12 fl oz) red wine
1 cup (250 ml/8 fl oz) chicken stock
1 teaspoon sugar
fresh coriander (cilantro) sprigs, to garnish

1 Crush the coriander seeds in a mortar and pestle. Combine the pork, crushed seeds and ½ teaspoon cracked pepper in a bowl. Cover and marinate overnight in the fridge.

2 Toss the flour and pork. Heat the oil in a large frying pan and cook the pork in batches over high heat for 1–2 minutes, or until brown. Remove.

3 Add the onion to the frying pan and cook over medium heat for 2–3 minutes, or until just golden. Return the meat to the pan, add the red wine, stock and sugar, and season. Bring to the boil, then reduce the heat and simmer, covered, for 1 hour.

4 Remove the meat. Return the pan to the heat and boil over high heat for 3–5 minutes, or until reduced and slightly thickened. Pour over the meat and top with the coriander.

INGREDIENTS

1 kg (2 lb) minced (ground) lamb
1 onion, finely chopped
2 cloves garlic, finely chopped
2 tablespoons finely chopped fresh flat-leaf parsley
2 tablespoons finely chopped fresh coriander (cilantro)
  leaves
$^1/_2$ teaspoon cayenne pepper
$^1/_2$ teaspoon ground allspice
$^1/_2$ teaspoon ground ginger
$^1/_2$ teaspoon ground cardamom
1 teaspoon ground cumin
1 teaspoon paprika

Sauce

2 tablespoons olive oil
1 onion, finely chopped
2 cloves garlic, finely chopped
2 teaspoons ground cumin
$^1/_2$ teaspoon ground cinnamon
1 teaspoon paprika
2 x 425 g (14 oz) cans chopped tomatoes
2 teaspoons harissa
$^1/_3$ cup (20 g/$^3/_4$ oz) chopped fresh coriander (cilantro)
  leaves

1   Preheat the oven to moderate 180°C (350°F/Gas 4). Lightly grease two baking trays.
    Place the lamb, onion, garlic, herbs and spices in a bowl, and mix together well. Season
    with salt and pepper. Roll tablespoons of the mixture into balls and place on the trays.
    Bake for 18–20 minutes, or until browned.

2   Meanwhile, to make the sauce, heat the oil in a large saucepan, add the onion and cook
    over medium heat for 5 minutes, or until soft. Add the garlic, cumin, cinnamon and paprika,
    and cook for 1 minute, or until fragrant.

3   Stir in the tomato and harissa, and bring to the boil. Reduce the heat and simmer for 20
    minutes, then add the meatballs and simmer for 10 minutes, or until cooked through. Stir in
    the coriander, season well, and serve.

INGREDIENTS

2 tablespoons olive oil

1 onion, finely chopped

3 cloves garlic, finely chopped

1 teaspoon ground ginger

1 teaspoon ground turmeric

2 teaspoons ground cumin

2 teaspoons ground cinnamon

$^1/_2$ teaspoon dried chilli flakes

400 g (14 oz) can diced tomatoes

400 g (14 oz) can chickpeas, rinsed and drained

$^1/_2$ cup (80 g/3 oz) sultanas

400 g (14 oz) butternut pumpkin (squash), peeled and cut into 3 cm (1 inch) cubes

2 large zucchini (courgettes) (250 g), cut into 2 cm ($^3/_4$ inch) pieces

2 carrots, cut into 2 cm ($^3/_4$ inch) pieces

1 cup (185 g/6$^1/_2$ oz) instant couscous

25 g butter

4 tablespoons chopped fresh mint

1   Heat the olive oil in a large saucepan over medium heat. Add the onion and cook for 3–5 minutes, or until translucent but not brown. Add the garlic, ginger, turmeric, cumin, cinnamon and chilli flakes, and cook for 1 minute. Add the tomato, chickpeas, sultanas and 1 cup (250 ml/8 fl oz) water. Bring to the boil, then reduce the heat and simmer, covered, for 20 minutes. Add the pumpkin, zucchini and carrot, and cook for a further 20 minutes, or until the vegetables are tender. Season with salt and black pepper.

2   Place the couscous in a large, heatproof bowl. Cover with 1 cup (250 ml/8 fl oz) boiling water and leave to stand for 5 minutes, or until all the water is absorbed. Fluff with a fork and stir in the butter and mint. Season with salt and ground black pepper, and serve with the stew.

INGREDIENTS

Sauce
1/2–1 teaspoon dashi granules
1/3 cup (80 ml/2 3/4 fl oz) soy sauce
2 tablespoons sake
2 tablespoons mirin
1 tablespoon caster sugar

300 g (10 oz) shirataki noodles (see note)
50 g (1 3/4 oz) lard
5 large spring onions, cut into 1 cm (1/2 inch) slices on the
    diagonal
16 fresh shiitake mushrooms, cut into smaller pieces if
    large
800 g (1 lb 10 oz) rump steak, thinly sliced across the grain
100 g (3 1/2 oz) watercress, trimmed
4 eggs (optional)

1 To make the sauce, dissolve the dashi granules in 1/2 cup (125 ml/4 fl oz) water. Add the soy sauce, sake, mirin and sugar, and stir until combined.

2 Drain the noodles, then soak them in boiling water for 2 minutes. Rinse in cold water and drain well.

3 Melt the lard in a large frying pan over medium heat. Cook the spring onion, mushrooms and beef in batches, stirring, for 1–2 minutes each batch, or until just brown. Return the meat, spring onion and mushrooms to the pan, then add the sauce and watercress. Cook for 1 minute, or until heated through and the watercress has wilted—the sauce needs to just cover the ingredients but not drown them.

4 To serve, divide the noodles among four serving bowls and spoon the sauce evenly over the top. If desired, crack an egg into each bowl and break up through the sauce using chopsticks until it partially cooks.

INGREDIENTS

300 g (10 oz) red mullet fillets

400 g (13 oz) firm white fish fillets

300 g (10 oz) cleaned calamari (squid)

1.5 litres (6¼ cups) fish stock

⅓ cup (80 ml/2¾ fl oz) olive oil

1 onion, chopped

6 cloves garlic, chopped

1 small fresh red chilli, chopped

1 teaspoon paprika

pinch saffron threads

150 ml (5 fl oz) white wine

425 g (14 oz) can crushed tomatoes

16 raw medium prawns (shrimp), peeled and deveined, tails
  intact

2 tablespoons brandy

24 black mussels, cleaned

1 tablespoon chopped fresh parsley

Picada

2 tablespoons olive oil

2 slices day-old bread, cubed

2 cloves garlic

5 blanched almonds, toasted

2 tablespoons fresh flat-leaf parsley

1 Cut the fish and calamari into 4 cm (1½ inch) pieces. Place the stock in a large saucepan, bring to the boil and boil for 15 minutes, or until reduced by half.

2 To make the picada, heat the oil in a frying pan, add the bread and cook, stirring, for 2–3 minutes, or until golden, adding the garlic for the last minute. Place the almonds, bread, garlic and parsley in a food processor and process, adding enough of the stock to make a smooth paste.

3 Heat 2 tablespoons of the oil in a large saucepan, add the onion, garlic, chilli and paprika, and cook, stirring, for 1 minute. Add the saffron, wine, tomato and stock. Bring to the boil, then reduce the heat and simmer.

4 Heat the remaining oil in a frying pan and quickly fry the fish and calamari for 3–5 minutes. Remove from the pan. Add the prawns, cook for 1 minute and then pour in the brandy. Carefully ignite the brandy with a match and let the flames burn down. Remove from the pan.

5 Add the mussels to the stock and simmer, covered, for 2–3 minutes, or until opened. Discard any that do not open. Add all the seafood and the picada to the pan, stirring until the sauce has thickened and the seafood has cooked through. Season to taste, sprinkle with the parsley, and serve.

INGREDIENTS

500 g (1 lb 2 oz) tiger prawns (shrimp)
1¹/₂ tablespoons lemon juice
3 tablespoons oil
¹/₂ onion, finely chopped
¹/₂ teaspoon ground turmeric
5 cm (2 inch) piece of cinnamon stick
4 cloves
7 cardamom pods
5 Indian bay leaves (cassia leaves)
2 cm (³/₄ inch) piece of ginger, grated
3 garlic cloves, chopped
1 teaspoon chilli powder
170 ml (²/₃ cup) coconut milk

1 Peel and devein the prawns, leaving the tails intact. Put them in a bowl, add the lemon juice, then toss together and leave for 5 minutes. Rinse the prawns under running cold water and pat dry with paper towels.

2 Heat the oil in a heavy-based frying pan and fry the onion until lightly browned. Add the turmeric, cinnamon, cloves, cardamom, bay leaves, ginger and garlic and fry for 1 minute. Add the chilli powder, coconut milk and salt, to taste, and slowly bring to the boil. Reduce the heat and simmer for 2 minutes.

3 Add the prawns, return to the boil, then reduce the heat and simmer for 5 minutes, or until the prawns are cooked through and the sauce is thick. (Care should be taken not to overcook the prawns or they will become rubbery.)

CREAMY PRAWN CURRY

97

BEEF BOURGUIGNONNE

1 kg (2 lb) topside or round steak
plain flour, seasoned with salt and pepper
3 rashers bacon, rind removed
1 tablespoon oil
12 pickling onions
1 cup (250 ml/8 fl oz) red wine
2 cups (500 ml/16 fl oz) beef stock
1 teaspoon dried thyme
200 g (6½ oz) button mushrooms
2 bay leaves

1 Trim the steak of fat and sinew and cut into 2 cm (¾ inch) cubes. Lightly toss in the seasoned flour to coat, shaking off the excess.

2 Cut the bacon into 2 cm (¾ inch) squares. Heat the oil in a large pan and quickly cook the bacon over medium heat. Remove the bacon from the pan, then add the meat and brown well in batches. Remove and set aside. Add the onions to the pan and cook until golden.

3 Return bacon and meat to pan with the remaining ingredients. Bring to the boil, reduce the heat and simmer, covered, for 1½ hours, or until the meat is very tender, stirring now and then. Remove the bay leaves to serve.

INGREDIENTS

1 orange
1 tablespoon olive oil
4 chicken breasts (skin and excess fat removed)
2 chorizo sausages (about 200 g/6½ oz), cut into 1 cm (½ inch) slices
1 cup (250 ml/8 fl oz) chicken stock
1 cup (250 g/8 oz) bottled tomato pasta sauce
12 Kalamata olives
Kalamata olives, extra, to garnish
fresh flat-leaf parsley, to garnish

1 Using a vegetable peeler, carefully cut 4 thin strips of orange rind (about 1 x 4 cm/½ x 1½ inches). Remove the peel and pith from the orange, and segment the flesh.

2 Heat the oil in a saucepan and brown the chicken and chorizo slices, in batches if necessary. (Leave the meat side of the chicken browning for 5 minutes.) Add the stock, tomato sauce and orange rind. Bring to the boil, then reduce the heat and simmer, covered, for 25 minutes.

3 Remove the lid, turn the chicken over and continue to simmer, uncovered, for about 25 minutes, or until the chicken is tender and the sauce reduced. Season with salt and freshly ground black pepper, and stir through the olives and orange segments. Garnish with extra olives and flat-leaf parsley.

INGREDIENTS

1 kg (2 lb) baby octopus
2 tablespoons olive oil
1 large onion, chopped
3 cloves garlic, crushed
1 bay leaf
3 cups (750 ml/24 fl oz) red wine
1/4 cup (60 ml/2 fl oz) red wine vinegar
400 g (13 oz) can crushed tomatoes
1 tablespoon tomato paste(purée)
1 tablespoon chopped fresh oregano
1/4 teaspoon ground cinnamon
small pinch ground cloves
1 teaspoon sugar
2 tablespoons finely chopped fresh flat-leaf parsley

1   Cut between the head and tentacles of the octopus, just below the eyes. Grasp the body and push the beak out and up through the centre of the tentacles with your fingers. Cut the eyes from the head by slicing off a small round. Discard the eye section. Carefully slit through one side, avoiding the ink sac, and remove any gut from inside. Rinse the octopus well under running water.

2   Heat the oil in a large saucepan, add the onion and cook over medium heat for 5 minutes, or until starting to brown. Add the garlic and bay leaf, and cook for 1 minute further. Add the octopus and stir to coat in the onion mixture.

3   Stir in the wine, vinegar, tomato, tomato paste, oregano, cinnamon, cloves and sugar. Bring to the boil, then reduce the heat and simmer for 1 hour, or until the octopus is tender and the sauce has thickened slightly. Stir in the parsley and season with salt and ground black pepper. Serve with a Greek salad and crusty bread to mop up the delicious juices.

INGREDIENTS

1.5 kg (3 lb) leg or shoulder of lamb, cut into 2.5 cm (1 inch) pieces

3 cloves garlic, chopped

⅓ cup (80 ml/2¾ fl oz) olive oil

2 teaspoons ground cumin

1 teaspoon ground ginger

1 teaspoon ground turmeric

1 teaspoon paprika

½ teaspoon ground cinnamon

2 onions, thinly sliced

600 ml (20 fl oz) beef stock

¼ preserved lemon, pulp discarded, rind rinsed and cut into thin strips

425 g (14 oz) can chickpeas, drained

35 g (1¼ oz) cracked green olives

¼ cup (15 g/½ oz) chopped fresh coriander (cilantro) leaves

1   Place the lamb pieces in a non-metallic bowl, add the chopped garlic, 2 tablespoons of the olive oil and the ground cumin, ginger, turmeric, paprika, cinnamon, and ½ teaspoon ground black pepper and 1 teaspoon salt. Mix well to coat, then leave to marinate for 1 hour.

2   Heat the remaining olive oil in a large saucepan, add the lamb in batches and cook over high heat for 2–3 minutes, or until browned. Remove from the pan. Add the onion and cook for 2 minutes, then return the meat to the pan and add the beef stock. Reduce the heat and simmer, covered, for 1 hour.

3   Add the preserved lemon strips, drained chickpeas and olives, and cook, uncovered, for a further 30 minutes, or until the lamb is tender and the sauce has reduced and thickened. Stir in the coriander. Serve in bowls with couscous.

CHILLI CON POLLO

1 tablespoon olive oil
1 onion, finely chopped
500 g (1 lb) minced (ground) chicken
1–2 teaspoons mild chilli powder
440 g (14 oz) can chopped tomatoes
2 tablespoons tomato paste (purée)
1–2 teaspoons soft brown sugar
425 g (14 oz) can red kidney beans, rinsed and drained

1   Heat the oil in a large saucepan. Add the chopped onion and cook over medium heat for
    3 minutes, or until soft. Increase the heat to high and add the chicken mince. Cook until
    the chicken has browned, breaking up any lumps with a wooden spoon.

2   Add the chilli powder to the chicken and cook for 1 minute. Stir in the tomato, tomato
    paste and $1/2$ cup (125 ml/4 fl oz) water.

3   Bring to the boil, then reduce the heat and simmer for 30 minutes. Stir through the sugar
    to taste and the kidney beans. Season. Serve with corn chips or in taco shells with sour
    cream.

INGREDIENTS

¼ cup (60 ml/2 fl oz) olive oil

4 chicken thighs and 6 drumsticks

1 large red onion, finely chopped

1 large green capsicum (pepper), two-thirds diced and one-third julienned

3 teaspoons sweet paprika

400 g (13 oz) can diced tomatoes

1¼ cups (275 g/9 oz) paella or arborio rice (see note)

½ teaspoon ground saffron

1 Heat 2 tablespoons of the oil in a large deep frying pan over high heat. Season the chicken pieces well and brown in batches. Remove the chicken from the pan.

2 Reduce the heat to medium and add the remaining oil. Add the onion and the diced capsicum, and cook gently for 5 minutes. Stir in the sweet paprika and cook for 30 seconds. Add the tomato and simmer for 1–3 minutes, or until it thickens.

3 Stir in 3½ cups (875 ml/28 fl oz) boiling water, then add the rice and saffron. Return the chicken to the pan and stir to combine. Season to taste. Bring to the boil, then cover, reduce the heat to medium–low and simmer for 20–30 minutes, or until the liquid has been absorbed and the chicken is tender. Stir in the julienned capsicum, then allow to stand, covered, for 3–4 minutes before serving.

NOTE Paella rice is a medium round grain from Spain. Calasparra is the most commonly available variety and can be purchased from fine food stores or Spanish delicatessens.

INGREDIENTS

100 ml (3^1/$_2$ fl oz) olive oil
1 large onion, finely chopped
2 cloves garlic, crushed
1 cup (80 g/2^3/$_4$ oz) fresh breadcrumbs
1 egg, lightly beaten
60 g (2 oz) kefalotyri cheese, grated
60 g (2 oz) haloumi cheese, grated
4 large or 8 small squid (1 kg/2 lb), cleaned (see note)
1 small onion, finely chopped, extra
2 cloves garlic, crushed, extra
500 g (1 lb) firm ripe tomatoes, peeled and diced
150 ml (5 fl oz) red wine
1 tablespoon chopped fresh oregano
1 tablespoon chopped fresh flat-leaf parsley

1 Heat 2 tablespoons of the oil in a frying pan, add the onion and cook over medium heat for 3 minutes. Remove. Combine with the garlic, breadcrumbs, egg and cheese. Season.

2 Pat the squid hoods dry with paper towels and, using a teaspoon, fill them three-quarters full with the stuffing. Do not pack them too tightly or the stuffing mixture will swell and burst out during cooking. Secure the ends with wooden toothpicks.

3 Heat the remaining oil in a large frying pan, add the squid and cook for 1–2 minutes on all sides. Remove. Add the extra onion and cook over medium heat for 3 minutes, or until soft, then add the extra garlic and cook for a further 1 minute. Stir in the tomato and wine, and simmer for 10 minutes, or until thick and pulpy, then stir in the oregano and parsley. Return the squid to the pan and cook, covered, for 20–25 minutes, or until tender. Serve warm with the tomato sauce or cool with a salad.

NOTE Ask the fishmonger to clean the squid. Or, discard the tentacles and cartilage. Rinse the hoods under running water and pull off the skin.

INGREDIENTS

350 g (11 oz) dried white haricot beans
150 g (5 oz) tocino, speck or pancetta, unsliced
$1/2$ leek, thinly sliced
2 cloves garlic
1 bay leaf
1 small fresh red chilli, halved and seeded
1 small onion
2 cloves
1 sprig fresh rosemary
3 sprigs fresh thyme
1 sprig fresh parsley
$1/4$ cup (60 ml/2 fl oz) olive oil
8 pork sausages
$1/2$ onion, finely chopped
1 green capsicum (pepper), finely chopped
$1/2$ teaspoon paprika
$1/2$ cup (125 ml/4 fl oz) tomato paste (purée)
1 teaspoon cider vinegar

1 Soak the beans overnight in cold water. Drain and rinse the beans under cold water. Put them in a large saucepan with the tocino, leek, garlic, bay leaf and chilli. Stud the onion with the cloves and add to the saucepan. Tie the rosemary, thyme and parsley together, and add to the saucepan. Pour in 3 cups (750 ml/24 fl oz) cold water and bring to the boil. Add 1 tablespoon of the oil, reduce the heat and simmer, covered, for about 1 hour, or until the beans are tender. When necessary, add a little more boiling water to keep the beans covered.

2 Prick each sausage 5 or 6 times and twist tightly in opposite directions in the middle to give 2 short fat sausages joined in the middle. Put in a single layer in a large frying pan and add enough cold water to reach halfway up their sides. Bring to the boil and simmer, turning two or three times, until all the water has evaporated and the sausages brown lightly in the little fat that is left in the pan. Remove from the pan and cut the short sausages apart. Add the remaining oil, the chopped onion and green capsicum to the pan, and fry over medium heat for 5–6 minutes. Stir in the paprika, cook for 30 seconds, then add the tomato purée. Season to taste. Cook, stirring, for 1 minute.

3 Remove the tocino, herb sprigs and any loose large pieces of onion from the bean mixture. Leave in any loose leaves from the herbs and any small pieces of onion. Add the sausages and sauce to the pan, and stir the vinegar through. Bring to the boil. Adjust the seasoning.

PORK SAUSAGE AND WHITE BEAN STEW

INGREDIENTS

2 tablespoons olive oil
4 duck breasts
2 red onions, finely diced
1 carrot, finely diced
2 teaspoons fresh thyme
1 cup (250 ml/8 fl oz) chicken stock
2 ripe tomatoes, peeled, seeded and diced
4 green, firm pears, peeled, halved and cored (leaving the stems intact)
1 cinnamon stick
60 g (2 oz) blanched almonds, toasted, chopped
1 clove garlic
100 ml (3^{1}/$_{2}$ fl oz) brandy

1 Heat the oil in a heavy-based frying pan and cook the duck, skin-side down first, over medium heat until brown all over. Remove and set aside, reserving 4 tablespoons of the cooking fat.

2 Return 2 tablespoons of the fat to the pan. Add the onion, carrot and thyme, and cook over medium heat for 5 minutes, or until the onion has softened. Add the stock and tomato and bring to the boil. Reduce the heat and simmer for 30 minutes, with the lid slightly askew, or until the sauce has thickened and reduced. Cool slightly, then purée in a food processor until smooth. Return to the pan with the duck. Simmer gently over low heat for 30–40 minutes, or until the duck is tender.

3 While the duck is cooking, place the pears in a saucepan with the cinnamon and just cover with cold water. Bring to the boil, reduce the heat and simmer gently for 5 minutes, or until the pears are tender but still firm to the bite. Remove the pears, cover to keep warm and add ^{1}/$_{2}$ cup (125 ml/4 fl oz) of the pear poaching liquid to the tomato sauce.

4 Remove the duck from the sauce and keep warm. Grind the almonds, garlic and brandy together in a mortar and pestle or blender to make a smooth paste. Add to the tomato sauce, season, and cook for another 10 minutes.

5 Arrange the duck pieces on a serving plate and pour the sauce over the top. Arrange the warmed pears around the duck, and serve.

NOTE The sauce adds an interesting finish to this Spanish dish, which is traditionally made with goose.

INGREDIENTS

1.5 kg (3 lb) black mussels
1/4 cup (60 ml/2 fl oz) olive oil
1 large onion, diced
4 cloves garlic, finely chopped
810 g (1 lb 10 oz) can diced tomatoes
1/4 cup (60 g/2 oz) tomato paste (purée)
1/4 cup (30 g/1 oz) pitted black olives
1 tablespoon capers
1/2 cup (125 ml/4 fl oz) fish stock
1/4 cup (7 g/1/4 oz) chopped fresh flat-leaf parsley

1 Scrub the mussels with a stiff brush and pull out the hairy beards. Discard any damaged mussels, or those that don't close when tapped on the bench.

2 In a large saucepan, heat the olive oil and cook the onion and garlic over medium heat for 1–2 minutes, until softened. Add the tomato, tomato paste, olives, capers and fish stock. Bring to the boil, then reduce the heat and simmer, stirring occasionally, for 20 minutes, or until the sauce is thick.

3 Stir in the mussels and cover the saucepan. Shake or toss the mussels occasionally, and cook for 4–5 minutes, or until the mussels begin to open. Once they have all opened, remove the pan from the heat. Discard any unopened mussels.

4 Just before serving, toss the parsley through. Serve with crusty bread.

MUSSEL AND TOMATO STEW

INGREDIENTS

250 g (8 oz) dried rice vermicelli

600 g (1¼ lb) lamb backstraps, thinly sliced across the grain

4 spring onions, sliced

1.5 litres light chicken stock

3 cm x 6 cm (1¼ inch x 2½ inch) piece fresh ginger, cut into 6 slices

2 tablespoons Chinese rice wine

300 g (10 oz) silken firm tofu, cut into 1.5 cm (⅝ inch) cubes

300 g (10 oz) Chinese broccoli, cut into 4 cm (1½ inch) lengths

2 cups (90 g/3 oz) shredded Chinese cabbage

Sauce

⅓ cup (80 ml/2¾ fl oz) light soy sauce

2 tablespoons Chinese sesame paste

1 tablespoon Chinese rice wine

1 teaspoon chilli and garlic paste

1 Place the vermicelli in a large heatproof bowl, cover with boiling water and soak for 6–7 minutes. Drain well and divide among six serving bowls. Top with the lamb slices and spring onion.

2 To make the sauce, combine the soy sauce, sesame paste, rice wine and the chilli and garlic paste in a small bowl.

3 Place the stock, ginger and rice wine in a 2.5 litre (10 cup) flameproof hotpot or large saucepan. Cover and bring to the boil over high heat. Add the tofu, Chinese broccoli and Chinese cabbage and simmer, uncovered, for 1 minute, or until the broccoli has wilted. Divide the tofu, broccoli and cabbage among the serving bowls, then ladle on the hot stock. Drizzle a little of the sauce on top and serve the rest on the side.

NOTE Make sure the stock is hot enough to cook the thin slices of lamb. This recipe traditionally uses a Chinese steamboat—this is an aluminium pot with a steam spout in the middle, placed on a propane burner in the middle of the dining table. You could use a fondue pot instead.

2 tablespoons olive oil
8 (1.2 kg/2 lb 6½ oz) chicken pieces
½ cup (125 ml/4 fl oz) chicken stock
½ cup (125 ml/4 fl oz) dry white wine
½ cup (125 ml/4 fl oz) balsamic vinegar
40 g (1¼ oz) chilled butter

1 Heat the oil in a large casserole dish over medium heat and cook the chicken, in batches, for 7–8 minutes, until browned. Pour off any excess fat.

2 Add the stock, bring to the boil, then reduce the heat and simmer, covered, for 30 minutes, or until the chicken is cooked through.

3 Add the white wine and vinegar and increase the heat to high. Boil for 1 minute, or until the liquid has thickened. Remove from the heat, stir in the butter until melted, and season. Spoon the sauce over the chicken to serve, accompanied by roast potatoes and salad.

NOTE Use a good-quality balsamic vinegar, as the cheaper varieties can be too acidic.

CHICKEN WITH BALSAMIC VINEGAR

INGREDIENTS

60 ml ($\frac{1}{4}$ cup) olive oil

1 large red capsicum (pepper), seeded and cut into 5 mm ($\frac{1}{4}$ inch) strips

600 g (1 lb 5 oz) chicken thigh fillets, cut into 3 cm (1$\frac{1}{4}$ inch) cubes

200 g (7 oz) chorizo sausage, cut into 2 cm ($\frac{3}{4}$ inch) slices

200 g (7 oz) mushrooms, thinly sliced

3 garlic cloves, crushed

1 tablespoon lemon zest

700 g (1 lb 9 oz) tomatoes, roughly chopped

200 g (7 oz) green beans, cut into 3 cm (1$\frac{1}{4}$ inch) lengths

1 tablespoon chopped rosemary

2 tablespoons chopped flat-leaf (Italian) parsley

$\frac{1}{4}$ teaspoon saffron threads dissolved in 60 ml ($\frac{1}{4}$ cup) hot water

440 g (2 cups) short-grain rice

750 ml (3 cups) hot chicken stock

6 lemon wedges

1 Heat the oil in a large deep frying pan or paella pan over medium heat. Add the capsicum and cook for 6 minutes, or until soft. Remove from the pan.

2 Add the chicken to the pan and cook for 10 minutes, or until brown on all sides. Remove. Add the sausage to the pan and cook for 5 minutes, or until golden on all sides. Remove.

3 Add the mushrooms, garlic and lemon zest and cook over medium heat for 5 minutes. Stir in the tomato and capsicum and cook for a further 5 minutes, or until the tomato is soft.

4 Add the beans, rosemary, parsley, saffron mixture, rice, chicken and sausage. Stir briefly and then add the stock. Do not stir at this point. Reduce the heat and simmer for 30 minutes. Remove the pan from the heat, cover and leave to stand for 10 minutes. Serve with lemon wedges.

NOTE Paellas are not stirred right to the bottom of the pan during cooking in the hope that a thin crust of crispy rice will form. This is considered one of the best parts of the paella. For this reason, do not use a non-stick frying pan. Paellas are traditionally served at the table from the pan.

INGREDIENTS

2 teaspoons ground cumin

1 teaspoon ground coriander (cilantro)

½ teaspoon chilli powder

¼ teaspoon ground cinnamon

400 g (13 oz) lean diced pork, trimmed

1 tablespoon plain (all-purpose) flour

1 tablespoon olive oil

1 large onion, finely chopped

3 cloves garlic, finely chopped

2 large carrots, chopped

2 celery sticks, sliced

½ cup (125 ml/4 fl oz) chicken stock

½ cup (125 ml/4 fl oz) beer

2 ripe tomatoes, chopped

310 g (10 oz) can chickpeas, rinsed

2 tablespoons chopped fresh parsley

1 Cook the spices in a dry frying pan over low heat, shaking the pan, for 1 minute, or until aromatic.

2 Combine the pork, trimmed of all fat, with the spices and flour in a plastic bag and toss well. Remove the pork and shake off the excess flour. Heat the oil in a large heavy-based pan over high heat and cook the pork, tossing regularly, for 8 minutes, or until lightly browned.

3 Add the onion, garlic, carrot, celery and half the stock to the pan and toss well. Cover and cook for 10 minutes. Add the remaining stock, beer and tomato and season to taste. Bring to the boil, reduce the heat, cover with a tight-fitting lid, then simmer over low heat for 1 hour. Gently shake the pan occasionally, but do not remove the lid during cooking. Stir in the chickpeas and fresh parsley. Simmer, uncovered, for 5 minutes and serve.

PORK, BEER AND CHICKPEA STEW

PROVENCALE OCTOPUS

1 kg (2 lb) baby octopus
$^{1}/_{4}$ cup (60 ml/2 fl oz) olive oil
1 large brown onion, chopped
2 cloves garlic
500 g (1 lb) ripe tomatoes, peeled, seeded and chopped
$1^{1}/_{3}$ cups (330 ml/11 fl oz) dry white wine
$^{1}/_{4}$ teaspoon saffron threads
2 sprigs fresh thyme
2 tablespoons roughly chopped fresh flat-leaf parsley

1 To clean the octopus, use a small sharp knife and cut each head from the tentacles. Remove the eyes by cutting a round of flesh from the base of each head. To clean the heads, carefully slit them open and remove the gut. Rinse thoroughly. Cut the heads in half. Push out the beaks from the centre of the tentacles from the cut side. Cut the tentacles into sets of four or two, depending on the size of the octopus.

2 Blanch all the octopus in boiling water for 2 minutes, then drain and allow to cool slightly. Pat dry with paper towels.

3 Heat the olive oil in a heavy-based frying pan and cook the onion for 7–8 minutes over medium heat until lightly golden. Add the octopus and garlic to the pan, and cook for another 2–3 minutes. Add the tomato, wine, saffron and thyme. Add just enough water to cover the octopus.

4 Simmer, covered, for 1 hour. Uncover and cook for another 15 minutes, or until the octopus is tender and the sauce has thickened a little. The cooking time will vary depending upon the size of the octopus. Season to taste. Serve hot or at room temperature, sprinkled with chopped parsley.

INGREDIENTS

1 cup (220 g/7 oz) dried chickpeas
1 kg (2 lb) chicken, trussed
500 g (1 lb) piece lean beef brisket
250 g (8 oz) piece smoke-cured bacon
125 g (4 oz) tocino, streaky bacon or speck
1 pig's trotter
200 g (6½ oz) chorizo
1 onion, studded with 2 cloves
1 bay leaf
1 morcilla blood sausage (optional)
250 g (8 oz) green beans, sliced lengthways
250 g (8 oz) green cabbage, cut into sections through the heart
300 g (10 oz) silverbeet leaves, stalks removed
4 small potatoes
2 leeks, cut into 10 cm (4 inch) lengths
pinch saffron threads
75 g (2½ oz) dried rice vermicelli

1   Soak the chickpeas in cold water overnight. Drain and rinse. Tie loosely in a muslin bag.

2   Put 3 litres cold water in a very large, deep saucepan. Add the chicken, beef, bacon and tocino, and bring
    to the boil. Add the chickpeas, pig's trotter and chorizo, return to the boil, then add the onion, bay leaf and
    ½ teaspoon salt. Simmer, partially covered, for 2½ hours.

3   After 2 hours, bring a saucepan of water to the boil, add the morcilla and gently boil for 5 minutes. Drain
    and set aside. Tie the green beans loosely in a muslin bag. Pour 1 litre (4 cups) water into a large
    saucepan and bring to the boil. Add the beans, cabbage, silverbeet, potatoes, leek and saffron with
    1 teaspoon of salt. Return to the boil and simmer for 30 minutes.

4   Strain the stock from both the meat and vegetable pans, and combine in a large saucepan. Bring to the
    boil, adjust the seasoning and add the vermicelli. Simmer for 6–7 minutes. Release the chickpeas and pile
    them in the centre of a large warm platter. Discard the tocino, then slice the meats and sausages.
    Arrange the meats and sausages in groups around the chickpeas at one end of the platter. Release the
    beans. Arrange the vegetables in groups around the other end. Spoon a little of the simmering broth
    (minus the vermicelli) over the meat, then pour the rest (with the vermicelli) into a soup tureen. Serve at
    once. It is traditional to serve the two dishes together, although the broth is eaten first.

SOBA NOODLES WITH MISO AND BABY EGGPLANT

250 g (9 oz) soba noodles
3 teaspoons dashi granules
1$^1/_2$ tablespoons yellow miso paste
1$^1/_2$ tablespoons Japanese soy sauce
1$^1/_2$ tablespoons mirin
2 tablespoons vegetable oil
$^1/_2$ teaspoon sesame oil
6 baby eggplants (aubergines), cut into 1 cm ($^1/_2$ inch) slices
2 garlic cloves, crushed
1 tablespoon finely chopped ginger
150 g (1 cup) cooked peas
2 spring onions (scallions), sliced thinly on the diagonal
toasted sesame seeds, to garnish

1 Cook the noodles in a large saucepan of boiling water for 5 minutes. Drain and refresh with cold water.

2 Dissolve the dashi granules in 375 ml (1$^1/_2$ cups) boiling water. Stir in the miso paste, soy sauce and mirin.

3 Heat half the oils in a large frying pan over high heat. Cook the eggplant in two batches, for 4 minutes, or until golden on both sides. (Use the remaining oil to cook the second batch of eggplant.)

4 Stir in the garlic and ginger, then the miso mixture and bring to the boil. Reduce the heat and simmer for 10 minutes, or until slightly thickened and the eggplant is cooked. Add the noodles and peas and cook for 2 minutes, or until heated through.

5 Serve the noodles in shallow bowls and garnish with spring onion and toasted sesame seeds.

INGREDIENTS

2 dried mushrooms
1 kg (2 lb) firm white fish fillets
375 g (12 oz) raw king prawns (jumbo shrimp)
1 raw lobster tail
12 mussels
1/4 cup (60 ml/2 fl oz) olive oil
1 large onion, finely chopped
1 green capsicum (pepper), finely chopped
2–3 cloves garlic, crushed
425 g (14 oz) can crushed tomatoes
1 cup (250 ml/8 fl oz) white wine
1 cup (250 ml/8 fl oz) tomato juice
1 cup (250 ml/8 fl oz) fish stock (see note)
1 bay leaf
2 sprigs fresh parsley
6 fresh basil leaves, chopped
1 tablespoon chopped fresh parsley

1   Soak the mushrooms in boiling water for 20 minutes. Cut the fish into bite-size pieces, removing any bones. Peel and devein the prawns, leaving the tails intact. Remove the meat from the lobster shell and cut into small pieces. Discard any open mussels; scrub the rest, remove the beards, then soak in cold water for 10 minutes. Drain the mushrooms, squeeze dry and chop finely.

2   Heat the oil in a heavy-based saucepan. Cook the onion, capsicum and garlic over medium heat, stirring, for about 5 minutes, or until the onion is soft. Add the mushrooms, tomato, wine, tomato juice, stock, bay leaf, parsley sprigs and chopped basil. Bring to the boil, reduce the heat, then cover and simmer for 30 minutes.

3   Layer the fish and prawns in a large pan. Add the sauce mixture, then cover and leave on low heat for 10 minutes, or until the prawns are pink and the fish is cooked. Add the lobster and mussels, and simmer for 2–3 minutes. Season to taste. Discard any unopened mussels, sprinkle with parsley, and serve with crusty bread.

NOTE   You can make your own fish stock for this recipe by simmering the trimmings from the fish, lobster and prawns in 1 1/4 cups (310 ml/10 fl oz) water for about 20 minutes, then straining the liquid.

INGREDIENTS

3 red capsicums
2.1 kg (4 lb 3 oz) frozen turkey hindquarters (legs with thighs), chopped (see notes)
seasoned plain (all-purpose) flour
$^1/_4$ cup (60 ml/2 fl oz) olive oil
60 g (2 oz) butter
$^3/_4$ cup (185 ml/6 fl oz) chicken stock
$^1/_4$ teaspoon dried chilli flakes
4 fresh sage leaves, chopped, or $^1/_2$ teaspoon dried sage
2 cloves garlic, crushed
1 teaspoon finely grated lemon rind
150 g (5 oz) sliced pancetta, or thinly sliced bacon
1 sprig fresh rosemary
2 tablespoons chopped fresh flat-leaf parsley

1 Preheat the grill to high. Cut the capsicums in half, then remove the seeds and membranes. Place the capsicum halves skin-side up under the grill and cook for 5–8 minutes, or until the skin blackens and blisters. Transfer to a plastic bag, seal and allow to cool, then peel away the blackened skin. Cut the flesh into thick slices.

2 Thaw the turkey pieces in a single layer in the refrigerator. When they have thawed, pat the turkey pieces well with paper towels to remove all the excess moisture, then coat them well in the seasoned flour, dusting off any excess.

3 Heat the oil and butter in a large saucepan. Brown the turkey pieces in batches over medium–high heat, then drain the pan of excess oil.

4 Pour the chicken stock into the pan and stir well, scraping the base and side of the pan to mix in all the pan juices. Add the chilli flakes, sage, garlic and lemon rind, and cook, stirring, for 1 minute.

5 Return all the turkey pieces to the pan. Cover with the grilled capsicum slices, then layer the pancetta over the top to completely cover. Add the rosemary sprig, cover the pan and cook over low heat for 1 hour, or until the turkey is succulent, yet not falling off the bone.

6 Discard the rosemary sprig and transfer the pancetta, capsicum slices and turkey pieces to a serving plate. Cover and keep warm. If the sauce is a little thin, place it over high heat and simmer for 3–4 minutes to thicken. Stir in the chopped parsley, adjust the seasoning if necessary, then spoon the sauce around the turkey to serve.

NOTE Ask your butcher or poulterer to saw the frozen turkey into 1.5–2 cm ($^3/_4$ inch) pieces for you. Pancetta is an Italian unsmoked bacon, rolled and cured with salt and spices, sold in many delicatessens. You could use prosciutto instead.

GREEN CURRY WITH SWEET POTATO AND EGGPLANT

GREEN CURRY WITH SWEET POTATO AND EGGPLANT

INGREDIENTS

1 tablespoon oil
1 onion, chopped
1–2 tablespoons green curry paste (see note)
1 eggplant (aubergine), quartered and sliced
1½ cups (375 ml/12 fl oz) coconut milk
1 cup (250 ml/8 fl oz) vegetable stock
6 kaffir lime (makrut) leaves
1 orange sweet potato (kumera), cubed
2 teaspoons soft brown sugar
2 tablespoons lime juice
2 teaspoons lime rind

1   Heat the oil in a large wok or frying pan. Add the onion and green curry paste and cook, stirring, over medium heat for 3 minutes. Add the eggplant and cook for a further 4–5 minutes, or until softened.

2   Pour in the coconut milk and vegetable stock, bring to the boil, then reduce the heat and simmer for 5 minutes. Add the kaffir lime leaves and sweet potato and cook for 10 minutes, or until the eggplant and sweet potato are very tender.

3   Mix in the sugar, lime juice and lime rind until well combined with the vegetables. Season to taste with salt and serve with steamed rice.

NOTE   Strict vegetarians should be sure to read the label and choose a green curry paste that doesn't contain shrimp paste. Alternatively, make your own curry pastes.

INGREDIENTS

¼ cup (60 ml/2 fl oz) oil
1 kg (2 lb) veal shoulder, diced
1 large onion, thinly sliced
3 cloves garlic, finely chopped
¼ cup (60 g/2 oz) Hungarian paprika
½ teaspoon caraway seeds
2 x 400 g (13 oz) cans chopped tomatoes, one drained
350 g (11 oz) fresh fettuccine
40 g (1¼ oz) butter, softened

1   Heat half the oil in a large saucepan over medium–high heat, then brown the veal in batches for 3 minutes per batch. Remove the veal from the pan and set aside with any pan juices.

2   Add the remaining oil to the pan and sauté the onion and garlic over medium heat for 5 minutes, or until softened. Add the paprika and ¼ teaspoon of the caraway seeds, and stir for 30 seconds.

3   Add the chopped tomatoes and their liquid plus ½ cup (125 ml/4 fl oz) water. Return the veal to the pan with any juices, increase the heat to high and bring to the boil. Reduce the heat to low, then cover and simmer for 1¼ hours, or until the meat is tender and the sauce has thickened.

4   About 15 minutes before the veal is ready, cook the pasta in a large saucepan of rapidly boiling salted water according to the packet instructions until al dente. Drain, then return to the pan. Stir in the butter and the remaining caraway seeds. Serve immediately with the paprika veal.

INGREDIENTS

¼ cup (60 ml/2 fl oz) olive oil
3 leeks, thinly sliced
1 teaspoon finely chopped fresh rosemary
3 bay leaves, torn
1 kg (2 lb) chicken pieces
seasoned plain (all-purpose) flour
1 large eggplant (aubergine), cut into cubes
2 zucchini (courgettes), roughly chopped
½ cup (125 ml/4 fl oz) Marsala
300 ml (10 fl oz) chicken stock
2 cups (500 ml/16 fl oz) tomato paste (purée)
200 g (6½ oz) button mushrooms, halved

1 Heat the oil in a large, heavy-based saucepan. Fry the leek, rosemary and bay leaves over low heat for 5 minutes, or until soft, stirring occasionally. Remove with a slotted spoon, leaving as much oil in the pan as possible.

2 Toss the chicken pieces in the seasoned flour. Add the chicken to the pan and brown well in batches over medium heat. Return all the chicken to the pan with the leek mixture.

3 Add the eggplant and zucchini, and cook, stirring, for 2–3 minutes, or until softened, turning the chicken over. Add the Marsala and stock, and cook for 15 minutes over medium–high heat.

4 Add the tomato purée and season well with salt and pepper. Bring to the boil, turning the chicken pieces in the sauce. Reduce the heat to a very gentle simmer, then cover and cook for 35 minutes. Add the mushrooms and cook, uncovered, for 5 minutes.

NOTE Marsala is a famous Italian fortified wine. It has a smoky, rich flavour and ranges from dry to sweet.

INGREDIENTS

300 g (10 oz) skinless firm white fish fillets (see note)

250 g (8 oz) black mussels

500 g (1 lb) raw medium prawns (shrimp), peeled and
  deveined, tails intact

200 g (6¹/₂ oz) calamari (squid) rings

¹/₄ cup (60 ml/2 fl oz) olive oil

1 large onion, diced

3 cloves garlic, finely chopped

1 small red capsicum (pepper), thinly sliced

1 small fresh red chilli, seeded and chopped (optional)

2 teaspoons paprika

1 teaspoon ground turmeric

2 tomatoes, peeled and diced

1 tablespoon tomato paste (purée)

2 cups (400 g/13 oz) long-grain rice

¹/₂ cup (125 ml/4 fl oz) white wine

1.25 litres fish stock

¹/₄ cup (7 g/1/4 oz) chopped fresh flat-leaf parsley, for
  serving

lemon wedges, for serving

1 Cut the fish fillets into 2.5 cm (1 inch) cubes. Scrub the mussels and pull out the hairy beards. Discard any broken mussels or those that don't close when tapped. Refrigerate the seafood, covered, until ready to use.

2 Heat the oil in a paella pan or a large deep frying pan with a lid. Add the onion, garlic, capsicum and chilli to the pan, and cook over medium heat for 2 minutes, or until the onion and capsicum are soft. Add the paprika, turmeric and 1 teaspoon salt, and stir-fry for 1–2 minutes, or until aromatic.

3 Add the tomato and cook for 5 minutes, or until softened. Add the tomato paste. Stir in the rice until it is well coated.

4 Pour in the wine and simmer until almost absorbed. Add all the fish stock and bring to the boil. Reduce the heat and simmer for 20 minutes, or until almost all the liquid is absorbed into the rice. There is no need to stir the rice, but you may occasionally wish to fluff it up with a fork to separate the grains.

5 Add the mussels to the pan, poking the shells into the rice, cover and cook for 2–3 minutes over low heat. Add the prawns and cook for 2–3 minutes. Add the fish, cover and cook for 3 minutes. Finally, add the calamari rings and cook for 1–2 minutes. By this time, the mussels should have opened—discard any unopened ones. The prawns should be pink and the fish should flake easily when tested with a fork. The calamari should be white, moist and tender. Cook for another 2–3 minutes if the seafood is not quite cooked, but avoid overcooking as the seafood will toughen and dry out.

6 Serve with parsley and lemon wedges. Delicious with a tossed salad.

NOTE You can use just fish, or other seafood such as scampi, octopus and crabs. If using just fish, choose one with few bones and chunky flesh, such as ling, blue-eye or warehou.

INGREDIENTS

1 cup (250 ml/8 fl oz) soy sauce
1 cinnamon stick
⅓ cup (90 g/3 oz) sugar
⅓ cup (80 ml/2¾ fl oz) balsamic vinegar
2.5 cm (1 inch) piece fresh ginger, thinly sliced
4 cloves garlic
¼ teaspoon dried chilli flakes
1.5 kg (3 lb) chicken pieces (skin removed)
1 tablespoon sesame seeds, toasted

1 Combine 1 litre water with the soy sauce, cinnamon stick, sugar, balsamic vinegar, ginger, garlic and chilli flakes in a saucepan. Bring to the boil, then reduce the heat and simmer for 5 minutes.

2 Add the chicken pieces and simmer, covered, for 50 minutes, or until cooked through. Serve the chicken on a bed of steamed greens, drizzled with the poaching liquid and sprinkled with toasted sesame seeds.

INGREDIENTS

2 tablespoons oil
8 (1.2 kg/2 lb 6½ oz) chicken pieces
1 onion, chopped
25 g (¾ oz) fresh oregano, leaves picked
2 tablespoons tomato paste (purée)
2 x 425 g (14 oz) cans crushed tomatoes
150 g (5 oz) black olives
150 g (5 oz) feta, crumbled

1 Heat half the oil in a saucepan and cook the chicken pieces, in batches, for 3–4 minutes, or until golden. Remove from the pan and set aside.

2 In the same saucepan, heat the reamining oil and cook the onion and half the oregano leaves for 3 minutes, or until the onion is soft. Add the tomato paste to the onion mixture and stir for 2 minutes, then add the tomato and the chicken pieces.

3 Simmer, covered, for 40–50 minutes, or until the chicken is cooked through. Add the olives and remaining oregano leaves. To serve, spoon into bowls and top with the crumbled feta.

CHILLI CON CARNE

185 g (6 oz) dried black eye beans
650 g (1 lb 5 oz) tomatoes
1½ tablespoons oil
900 g (1 lb 13 oz) trimmed chuck steak, cut into chunks
3 onions, thinly sliced
2 cloves garlic, chopped
2 teaspoons ground cumin
1 tablespoon paprika
½ teaspoon ground allspice
1–2 teaspoons chilli powder
1 tablespoon soft brown sugar
1 tablespoon red wine vinegar

1 Put the beans in a bowl, cover with plenty of water and leave overnight to soak. Drain well. Score a cross in the base of each tomato. Put the tomatoes in a bowl of boiling water for 30 seconds, then transfer to a bowl of cold water. Drain and peel the skin away from the cross. Halve the tomatoes and remove the seeds with a teaspoon. Chop the flesh finely.

2 Heat 1 tablespoon of the oil in a large heavy-based pan and add half the meat. Cook over medium-high heat for 2 minutes, or until well browned. Remove from the pan and repeat with the remaining meat, then remove from the pan.

3 Add the rest of the oil to the pan and add the onion. Cook over medium heat for 5 minutes, or until softened. Add the garlic and spices and cook, stirring, for 1 minute, or until aromatic. Add 2 cups (500 ml/16 fl oz) water and stir. Return the meat to the pan with the beans and tomatoes. Bring to the boil, then reduce the heat to low and simmer, partially covered, for 2 hours, or until the meat is tender and the chilli con carne is thick and dryish, stirring occasionally. Towards the end of the cooking time the mixture may start to catch, so add a little water if necessary. Stir through the sugar and vinegar, and season with salt to taste. Serve with flour tortillas, grated low-fat cheese and lime wedges.

INGREDIENTS

60 ml ($^1/_4$ cup) olive oil
4 chicken thighs and 6 drumsticks
1 large red onion, finely chopped
1 large green capsicum (pepper), two-thirds diced and one-third julienned
3 teaspoons sweet paprika
400 g (14 oz) can chopped tomatoes
250 g (1$^1/_4$ cups) long-grain rice
$^1/_2$ teaspoon ground saffron

1   Heat 2 tablespoons of the oil in a deep frying pan over high heat. Season the chicken pieces well and brown in batches. Remove the chicken from the pan.

2   Reduce the heat to medium and add the remaining oil. Add the onion and diced capsicum, and cook gently for 5 minutes. Stir in the paprika and cook for about 30 seconds. Add the tomato and simmer for 1–3 minutes, or until the mixture thickens.

3   Stir 875 ml (3$^1/_2$ cups) of boiling water into the pan, then add the rice and saffron. Return the chicken to the pan and stir to combine. Season with salt and pepper. Bring to the boil, cover, reduce the heat to medium–low and simmer for 20 minutes, or until all the liquid has been absorbed and the chicken is tender. Stir in the julienned capsicum, then allow it to stand, covered, for 3–4 minutes before serving.

PORK, PAPRIKA AND POTATO STEW

1 tablespoon paprika
4 thick pork loin cutlets
2 tablespoons olive oil
¼ cup (60 ml/2 fl oz) sherry vinegar
¼ teaspoon cayenne pepper
½ cup (125 ml/4 fl oz) tomato purée
400 g (13 oz) potatoes, cut into 2 cm (¾ inch) cubes
8 French shallots, peeled
200 g (6½ oz) rocket leaves

1 Combine the paprika with ¼ teaspoon each of salt and freshly ground black pepper. Sprinkle over both sides of the pork. Heat the oil over medium heat in a deep frying pan large enough to fit the cutlets in a single layer, and cook the cutlets until brown on both sides.

2 Pour the sherry vinegar into the pan and stir well to scrape up any sediment stuck to the base. Stir in the cayenne pepper, tomato purée and 1 cup (250 ml/8 fl oz) hot water. Bring to the boil, then add the potato and shallots. Reduce the heat and simmer, covered, for 30 minutes, or until the sauce has thickened and reduced by half—check the liquid level once or twice, and add a little more water if necessary. Season.

3 To serve, divide the rocket leaves among four serving plates and place a cutlet on top. Spoon the sauce and potato over the top.

INGREDIENTS

2 tablespoons olive oil

1 large red onion, finely chopped

1 garlic clove, crushed

2 back bacon rashers, finely chopped

300 g (1¹/₂ cups) long-grain rice

1 red capsicum (pepper), diced

150 g (5¹/₂ oz) ham, chopped

400 g (14 oz) can chopped tomatoes

400 g (14 oz) tomato passata or tomato pasta sauce

1 teaspoon Worcestershire sauce

dash of Tabasco sauce

¹/₂ teaspoon dried thyme

30 g (¹/₂ cup) chopped parsley

150 g (5¹/₂ oz) cooked, peeled, small prawns (shrimp)

4 spring onions (scallions), thinly sliced

1 Heat the oil in a large saucepan over medium heat. Add the onion, garlic and bacon and cook, stirring, for 5 minutes, or until the onion is softened but not browned. Stir in the rice and cook for a further 5 minutes, or until lightly golden.

2 Add the capsicum, ham, tomatoes, tomato passata, Worcestershire and Tabasco sauces and thyme and stir until well combined. Bring the mixture to the boil, then reduce the heat to low. Cook, covered, for 30–40 minutes, or until the rice is tender.

3 Stir in the parsley and prawns and season with salt and freshly ground black pepper. Sprinkle with the spring onion, then serve.

CHINESE BEEF IN SOY

700 g (1 lb 7 oz) chuck steak, trimmed and cut into 2 cm (1 inch) cubes
⅓ cup (80 ml/2¾ fl oz) dark soy sauce
2 tablespoons honey
1 tablespoon wine vinegar
3 tablespoons soy bean oil
4 cloves garlic, chopped
8 spring onions, finely sliced
1 tablespoon finely grated fresh ginger
2 star anise
½ teaspoon ground cloves
1½ cups (375 ml/12 fl oz) beef stock
½ cup (125 ml/4 fl oz) red wine
spring onions, extra, sliced, to garnish

1 Place the meat in a non-metallic dish. Combine the soy sauce, honey and vinegar in a small bowl, then pour over the meat. Cover with plastic wrap and marinate for at least 2 hours, or preferably overnight. Drain, reserving the marinade, and pat the cubes dry.

2 Place 1 tablespoon of the oil in a saucepan and brown the meat in 3 batches, for 3–4 minutes per batch— add another tablespoon of oil, if necessary. Remove the meat. Add the remaining oil and fry the garlic, spring onion, ginger, star anise and cloves for 1–2 minutes, or until fragrant.

3 Return all the meat to the pan, add the reserved marinade, stock and wine. Bring to the boil and simmer, covered, for 1 hour 15 minutes. Cook, uncovered, for a further 15 minutes, or until the sauce is syrupy and the meat is tender.

4 Garnish with the extra sliced spring onion and serve immediately with rice.

INGREDIENTS

70 g (2¹/₂ oz) cellophane noodles (mung bean vermicelli)

250 g (9 oz) Chinese cabbage

1 litre (4 cups) chicken stock

2.5 x 2.5 cm (1 x 1 inch) piece ginger, thinly sliced

350 g (12 oz) Chinese roast pork, skin removed and reserved (see note)

2 spring onions (scallions), thinly sliced on the diagonal

2 tablespoons light soy sauce

1 tablespoon Chinese rice wine

¹/₂ teaspoon sesame oil

1 Soak the noodles in boiling water for 3–4 minutes. Drain and rinse, then drain again.

2 Separate the cabbage leaves and cut the leafy ends from the stems. Cut both the cabbage stems and leaves into 2–3 cm (³/₄–1¹/₄ inch) squares.

3 Place the stock and ginger slices in a 2 litre (8 cup) flameproof casserole dish and bring to the boil over high heat. Add the cabbage stems and cook for 2 minutes, then add the cabbage leaves and cook for 1 minute. Reduce the heat to medium, add the noodles and cook, covered, for 4–5 minutes, stirring occasionally.

4 Meanwhile, cut the pork into 2 cm (³/₄ inch) cubes and add the spring onion, soy sauce, rice wine and sesame oil. Stir to combine, then cook, covered, for 3–4 minutes and then serve.

NOTE If desired, grill (broil) the reserved pork skin for 1 minute, or until crispy, and arrange on top of each serving.

INGREDIENTS

50 g (1¾ oz) butter
2 tablespoons olive oil
250 g (8 oz) piece double-smoked ham, cut into cubes (see note)
3 cloves garlic, finely chopped
3 leeks, sliced
1.5 kg (3 lb) potatoes, peeled and cut into large chunks
2 cups (500 ml/16 fl oz) chicken stock
2 tablespoons brandy
½ cup (125 ml/4 fl oz) cream
1 tablespoon each of chopped fresh oregano and parsley

1   Heat the butter and oil in a large heavy-based saucepan. Cook the ham, garlic and leek over low heat for 10 minutes, stirring regularly.

2   Add the potato and cook for 10 minutes, stirring regularly.

3   Slowly stir in the combined stock and brandy. Cover and bring to a gentle simmer. Cook for another 15–20 minutes, or until the potato is very tender but still chunky, and the sauce has thickened. Add the cream and herbs, and season with salt and pepper. Simmer for another 5 minutes. Serve with toast.

NOTE   You can use any type of ham for this recipe. A double-smoked ham will give a good flavour.

INGREDIENTS

300 g (10 oz) beef fillet, trimmed
1.5 litres chicken stock
2 cm x 6 cm (³/₄ inch x 2¹/₂ inch) piece fresh ginger, thinly sliced
¹/₃ cup (80 ml/2³/₄ fl oz) light soy sauce
2 tablespoons mirin
1 teaspoon sesame oil
200 g (6¹/₂ oz) fresh udon noodles
150 g (5 oz) English spinach, stems removed, thinly sliced
400 g (13 oz) Chinese cabbage (leaves only), finely shredded
100 g (3¹/₂ oz) fresh shiitake mushrooms, stems removed and caps thinly sliced
200 g (6¹/₂ oz) firm tofu, cut into 2 cm (³/₄ inch) cubes
¹/₃ cup (80 ml/2³/₄ fl oz) ponzu sauce, or ¹/₄ cup (60 ml/2 fl oz) soy sauce combined with 1 tablespoon lemon juice

1   Wrap the beef fillet in plastic wrap and freeze for 40 minutes, or until it begins to harden. Remove and slice as thinly as possible across the grain.

2   Place the stock, ginger, soy sauce, mirin and sesame oil in a 2.5 litre (10 cup) flameproof casserole dish or hotpot over medium heat, and simmer for 3 minutes. Add the noodles, stir to separate gently with chopsticks and cook for 1–2 minutes. Add the spinach, cabbage, mushrooms and tofu, and simmer for 1 minute, or until the leaves have wilted.

3   Divide the noodles among four serving bowls using tongs, and top with the beef slices, vegetables and tofu. Ladle the hot stock on top and serve the ponzu sauce on the side.

NOTE   Traditionally, raw beef slices are arranged on a plate with the tofu, mushrooms, vegetables and noodles. The stock and seasoning are heated on a portable gas flame at the table. Guests dip the meat and vegetables in the hot stock and eat as they go, dipping into the dipping sauce. The noodles are added at the end and served with the broth.

MEE GROB

4 Chinese dried mushrooms

oil, for deep-frying

100 g (3½ oz) dried rice vermicelli

100 g (3½ oz) fried tofu, cut into matchsticks

4 garlic cloves, crushed

1 onion, chopped

1 chicken breast fillet, thinly sliced

8 green beans, sliced on the diagonal

6 spring onions (scallions), thinly sliced on the diagonal

8 raw prawns (shrimp), peeled and deveined, with tails
   intact

30 g (⅓ cup) bean sprouts

coriander (cilantro) leaves, to garnish

Sauce

1 tablespoon soy sauce

3 tablespoons white vinegar

5 tablespoons sugar

3 tablespoons fish sauce

1 tablespoon sweet chilli sauce

1 Soak the mushrooms in boiling water for 20 minutes. Drain, discard the stems and thinly slice.

2 Fill a wok one-third full of oil and heat to 180°C (350°F), or until a cube of bread browns in 15 seconds. Cook the vermicelli in small batches for 5 seconds, or until puffed and crispy. Drain. Add the tofu to the wok in batches and deep-fry for 1 minute, or until crisp. Drain. Carefully remove all but 2 tablespoons of oil.

3 Reheat the wok until very hot and add the garlic and onion and stir-fry for 1 minute. Add the chicken pieces, mushrooms, beans and half the spring onion. Stir-fry for 2 minutes, or until the chicken has almost cooked through. Add the prawns and stir-fry for a further 2 minutes, or until they just turn pink.

4 Combine all the sauce ingredients and add to the wok. Stir-fry for 2 minutes, or until the meat and prawns are tender and the sauce is syrupy.

5 Remove from the heat and stir in the vermicelli, tofu and bean sprouts. Garnish with the coriander and remaining sliced spring onion.

INGREDIENTS

1 tablespoon oil
1 onion, chopped
1–2 tablespoons green curry paste
1$\frac{1}{2}$ cups (375 ml/12 fl oz) coconut milk
500 g (1 lb) chicken thigh fillets, cut into bite-sized pieces
100 g (3$\frac{1}{2}$ oz) green beans, cut into short pieces
6 kaffir lime (makrut) leaves
1 tablespoon fish sauce
1 tablespoon lime juice
1 teaspoon finely grated lime rind
2 teaspoons soft brown sugar
$\frac{1}{4}$ cup (7 g/$\frac{1}{4}$ oz) fresh coriander (cilantro) leaves

1 Heat the oil in a wok or a heavy-based pan. Add the onion and curry paste to the wok and cook for about 1 minute, stirring constantly. Add the coconut milk and $\frac{1}{2}$ cup (125 ml/4 fl oz) water and bring to the boil.

2 Add the chicken pieces, beans and kaffir lime leaves to the wok, and stir to combine. Simmer, uncovered, for 15–20 minutes, or until the chicken is tender. Add the fish sauce, lime juice, lime rind and brown sugar to the wok, and stir to combine. Sprinkle with fresh coriander leaves just before serving. Serve with steamed rice.

NOTE Chicken thigh fillets are sweet in flavour and a very good texture for curries. You can use breast fillets instead, if you prefer. Do not overcook fillets or they will be tough.

INGREDIENTS

450 g (1 lb) sirloin steak, cut into thin strips
125 ml ($^1/_2$ cup) teriyaki marinade
vegetable oil, for deep-frying
100 g ($3^1/_2$ oz) dried rice vermicelli
2 tablespoons peanut oil
1 onion, sliced
3 garlic cloves, crushed
1 red chilli, seeded and finely chopped
200 g (7 oz) carrots, julienned
600 g (1 lb 5 oz) choy sum, cut into 3 cm ($1^1/_4$ inch) lengths
1 tablespoon lime juice

1   Combine the beef and teriyaki marinade in a non-metallic bowl and marinate for 2 hours.

2   Fill a wok one-third full of oil and heat to 190°C (375°F), or until a cube of bread browns in 10 seconds. Separate the vermicelli noodles into small bundles and deep-fry until they sizzle and puff up. Drain well on paper towels. Drain the oil and carefully pour it into a heatproof bowl to cool before discarding.

3   Heat 1 tablespoon of the peanut oil in the wok. When the oil is nearly smoking, add the beef (reserving the marinade) and cook in batches over high heat for 1–2 minutes. Remove to a plate. Heat the remaining oil. Add the onion and stir-fry for 3–4 minutes. Add the garlic and chilli and cook for 30 seconds. Add the carrot and choy sum and stir-fry for 3–4 minutes, or until tender.

4   Return the beef to the wok with the lime juice and reserved marinade and cook over high heat for 3 minutes. Add the noodles, toss well briefly, and serve immediately.

INGREDIENTS

3 tablespoons olive oil
850 g (1 lb 14 oz) Italian sausages
1 onion, chopped
3 garlic cloves, thinly sliced
1¹/₂ tablespoons chopped rosemary
2 x 400 g (14 oz) cans chopped tomatoes
16 juniper berries, lightly crushed
pinch of grated nutmeg
1 bay leaf
1 dried chilli, crushed
185 ml (³/₄ cup) red wine
100 g (¹/₂ cup) green lentils

1 Heat the oil in a large saucepan and cook the sausages for 5–10 minutes, until browned. Remove the sausages from the pan and reduce the heat. Add the onion and garlic to the pan and cook gently until the onion is soft.

2 Stir in the rosemary and then add the tomato and cook gently until reduced to a thick sauce. Add the juniper berries, nutmeg, bay leaf, chilli, wine and 420 ml (1²/₃ cups) water. Bring to the boil, then add the lentils and sausages. Give the stew a good stir, cover the pan and simmer gently for about 40 minutes, or until the lentils are soft. Stir a couple of times to prevent the lentils sticking to the base of the pan. Add a little more water if the lentils are still not cooked.

INGREDIENTS

1 kg (2 lb 4 oz) diced beef
30 g ('/₄ cup) plain (all-purpose) flour, seasoned
1 tablespoon oil
150 g (5¹/₂ oz) bacon, diced
8 bulb spring onions (scallions), greens trimmed to 2 cm (³/₄ inch)
200 g (7 oz) button mushrooms
500 ml (2 cups) red wine
2 tablespoons tomato paste (purée)
500 ml (2 cups) beef stock
bouquet garni (see note)

1 Toss the beef in the flour until evenly coated, shaking off any excess. Heat the oil in a large saucepan over high heat. Cook the beef in three batches for about 3 minutes, or until well browned all over, adding a little extra oil as needed. Remove from the pan.

2 Add the bacon and cook for 2 minutes, or until browned. Remove with a slotted spoon and add to the beef. Add the spring onions and mushrooms and cook for 5 minutes, or until the onions are browned. Remove.

3 Slowly pour the red wine into the pan, scraping up any sediment from the bottom with a wooden spoon. Stir in the tomato paste and stock. Add the bouquet garni and return the beef, bacon and any juices. Bring to the boil, then reduce the heat and simmer for 45 minutes, then return the spring onions and mushrooms to the pan. Cook for 1 hour, or until the meat is tender and the sauce is glossy. Serve with steamed new potatoes or mash.

NOTE To make a bouquet garni, wrap the green part of a leek around a bay leaf, a sprig of thyme, a sprig of parsley and celery leaves, and tie with string. The combination of herbs can be varied according to taste.

INGREDIENTS

16 mussels
12 large prawns (shrimp)
435 ml (1³/₄ cups) cider or dry white wine
50 g (1³/₄ oz) butter
1 garlic clove, crushed
2 shallots, finely chopped
2 celery stalks, finely chopped
1 large leek, white part only, thinly sliced
250 g (9 oz) small chestnut mushrooms, sliced
1 bay leaf
300 g (10¹/₂ oz) salmon fillet, skinned and cut into chunks
400 g (14 oz) sole fillet, skinned and cut into thick strips widthways
300 ml (10¹/₂ fl oz) thick (double/heavy) cream
3 tablespoons finely chopped parsley

1 Scrub the mussels and remove their beards. Throw away any that are open and don't close when tapped on the bench. Peel and devein the prawns.

2 Pour the cider into a large saucepan and bring to a simmer. Add the mussels, cover the pan and cook for 3–5 minutes, shaking the pan every now and then. Place a fine sieve over a bowl, tip in the mussels, then transfer them to a plate, throwing away any that haven't opened. Strain the cooking liquid again through the sieve.

3 Add the butter to the cleaned saucepan and melt over moderate heat. Add the garlic, shallot, celery and leek and cook for 7–10 minutes, or until the vegetables are just soft. Add the mushrooms and cook for a further 4–5 minutes until softened. While the vegetables are cooking, remove the mussels from their shells.

4 Add the strained liquid to the vegetables in the saucepan, add the bay leaf and bring to a simmer. Add the salmon, sole and prawns and cook for 3–4 minutes until the fish is opaque and the prawns are pink. Stir in the cream and cooked mussels and simmer for 2 minutes. Season and stir in the parsley.

INGREDIENTS

10 pieces veal shank, about 4 cm (1$\frac{1}{2}$ inch) thick
plain (all-purpose) flour, seasoned with salt and pepper
60 ml ($\frac{1}{4}$ cup) olive oil
60 g (2$\frac{1}{4}$ oz) butter
1 garlic clove
1 small carrot, finely chopped
1 large onion, finely chopped
$\frac{1}{2}$ celery stalk, finely chopped
250 ml (1 cup) dry white wine
375 ml (1$\frac{1}{2}$ cups) veal or chicken stock
400 g (14 oz) can chopped tomatoes
bouquet garni

1 Tie each piece of veal shank around its girth to secure the flesh, then dust with the seasoned flour. Heat the oil, butter and garlic in a large heavy saucepan big enough to hold the shanks in a single layer. Put the shanks in the saucepan and cook for 12–15 minutes until well browned. Remove the shanks from the pan and set aside. Discard the garlic.

2 Add the carrot, onion and celery to the pan and cook over moderate heat for 5–6 minutes, without browning. Increase the heat to high, add the wine and cook for 2–3 minutes. Add the stock, tomatoes and bouquet garni. Season with salt and pepper.

3 Return the veal shanks to the pan, standing them up in a single layer. Cover the pan, reduce the heat and simmer for 1 hour, or until the meat is tender and you can cut it with a fork.

4 If you prefer a thicker sauce, remove the veal shanks and increase the heat. Boil the sauce until reduced and thickened, then return the veal to the saucepan. Discard the bouquet garni, and taste for salt and pepper. If desired, serve with mashed potato.

INGREDIENTS

1¹/₂ tablespoons peanut oil

1 kg (2 lb 4 oz) stewing beef (such as chuck), cut into 3 cm (1¹/₄ inch) cubes

1 tablespoon finely chopped ginger

1 tablespoon finely chopped garlic

1 litre (4 cups) good-quality beef stock

80 ml (¹/₃ cup) Chinese rice wine

80 ml (¹/₃ cup) hoisin sauce

5 cm (2 inch) piece cassia bark

1 piece dried tangerine peel

1 star anise

1 teaspoon Sichuan peppercorns, lightly crushed

2 teaspoons soft brown sugar

300 g (10¹/₂ oz) daikon, cut into 3 cm (1¹/₄ inch) chunks

3 spring onions (scallions), cut into 3 cm (1¹/₄ inch) lengths, plus extra, to garnish

50 g (1³/₄ oz) sliced bamboo shoots

a few drops sesame oil (optional)

1 Heat a wok until very hot, add the peanut oil and swirl to coat the side. Stir-fry the beef in four batches for 1–2 minutes for each batch, or until the meat is browned all over. Remove from the wok.

2 Add the ginger and garlic to the wok and stir-fry for a few seconds. Add the stock, rice wine, hoisin sauce, cassia bark, tangerine peel, star anise, Sichuan peppercorns, sugar, daikon and 875 ml (3¹/₂ cups) water, then return the beef to the wok.

3 Bring to the boil, skimming any scum that forms on the surface, then reduce to a simmer and cook, stirring occasionally, for 1¹/₂ hours, or until the beef is tender and the sauce has thickened slightly. Add the spring onion and bamboo shoots 5 minutes before the end of the cooking time. Stir in a few drops of sesame oil, if desired, and garnish with extra spring onion. Serve with rice.

NOTE You can remove the star anise, cassia bark and tangerine peel before serving or leave them in the serving dish for presentation.

CHICKEN CASSEROLE WITH MUSTARD AND TARRAGON

1/4 cup (60 ml/2 fl oz) olive oil

1 kg (2 lb) chicken thigh fillets, halved, then quartered

1 onion, finely chopped

1 leek, sliced

1 clove garlic, finely chopped

350 g (12 1/2 oz) button mushrooms, sliced

1/2 teaspoon dried tarragon

1 1/2 cups (375 ml/12 1/2 fl oz) chicken stock

3/4 cup (185 ml/6 1/4 fl oz) cream

2 teaspoons lemon juice

2 teaspoons Dijon mustard

1 Preheat the oven to moderate 180°C (350°F/ Gas 4). Heat 1 tablespoon of the oil in a flameproof casserole dish over medium heat, and cook the chicken in two batches for 6–7 minutes each, or until golden. Remove from the dish.

2 Add the remaining oil to the casserole dish and cook the onion, leek and garlic over medium heat for 5 minutes, or until soft. Add the mushrooms and cook for 5–7 minutes, or until they are soft and browned, and most of the liquid has evaporated. Add the tarragon, chicken stock, cream, lemon juice and mustard, bring to the boil and cook for 2 minutes. Return the chicken pieces to the dish and season well. Cover.

3 Place the casserole in the oven and cook for 1 hour, or until the sauce has reduced and thickened. Season to taste with salt and pepper, and serve with potatoes and a green salad.

INGREDIENTS

4 pieces (500 g/1 lb 2 oz) veal schnitzel
plain (all-purpose) flour, seasoned
50 g (1³/₄ oz) butter
1 tablespoon oil
185 ml (³/₄ cup) dry Marsala
3 teaspoons cream
30 g (1 oz) butter, chopped, extra

1 Using a meat mallet or the heel of your hand, flatten the schnitzel pieces to 5 mm (¹/₄ inch) thick. Dust the veal in the flour, shaking off any excess. Heat the butter and oil in a large frying pan and cook the veal over medium–high heat for 1–2 minutes on each side, or until almost cooked through. Remove and keep warm.

2 Add the Marsala to the pan and bring to the boil, scraping the base of the pan to loosen any sediment. Reduce the heat and simmer for 1–2 minutes, or until slightly reduced. Add the cream and simmer for 2 minutes, then whisk in the extra butter until the sauce thickens slightly. Return the veal to the pan and simmer for 1 minute, or until the meat is warmed through. Serve immediately. Delicious with a creamy garlic mash and a tossed green salad.

NOTE Purchase veal that is pale in colour and free of sinew. Sinew will make the meat tough.

INGREDIENTS

400 g (14 oz) beef fillet, cut into 1 x 5 cm ($^1/_2$ x 2 inch) strips
2 tablespoons plain (all-purpose) flour
50 g (1$^3/_4$ oz) butter
1 onion, thinly sliced
1 garlic clove, crushed
250 g (9 oz) small Swiss brown mushrooms, sliced
60 ml ($^1/_4$ cup) brandy
250 ml (1 cup) beef stock
1$^1/_2$ tablespoons tomato paste (purée)
185 g ($^3/_4$ cup) sour cream
1 tablespoon chopped flat-leaf (Italian) parsley

1   Dust the beef strips in flour, shaking off any excess.

2   Melt half the butter in a large frying pan and cook the meat in small batches for 1–2 minutes, or until seared all over. Remove. Add the remaining butter to the pan and cook the onion and garlic over medium heat for 2–3 minutes, or until they soften. Add the mushrooms and cook for 2–3 minutes.

3   Pour in the brandy and simmer until nearly all of the liquid has evaporated, then stir in the beef stock and tomato paste. Cook for 5 minutes to reduce the liquid slightly. Return the beef strips to the pan with any juices and stir in the sour cream. Simmer for 1 minute, or until the sauce thickens slightly. Season with salt and freshly ground black pepper.

4   Garnish with the chopped parsley and serve immediately with fettucine or steamed rice.

INGREDIENTS

20 g ($^3/_4$ oz) butter
1 tablespoon vegetable oil
8 lamb neck chops, trimmed
4 rashers bacon, cut into strips
1 teaspoon plain (all-purpose) flour
600 g (1 lb 5 oz) potatoes, peeled and cut into thick slices
3 carrots, cut into thick slices
1 onion, cut into 16 wedges
1 small leek, cut into thick slices
150 g (5$^1/_2$ oz) savoy cabbage, thinly sliced
500 ml (2 cups) beef stock
2 tablespoons finely chopped flat-leaf (Italian) parsley

1 Heat the butter and oil in a flameproof casserole dish or a large heavy-based saucepan over high heat. Add the chops and cook for 1–2 minutes on each side, or until browned, then remove from the dish. Add the bacon and cook for 2–3 minutes, or until crisp. Remove with a slotted spoon, leaving the drippings in the dish.

2 Sprinkle the flour into the dish and stir to combine. Remove from the heat and layer half the potato, carrot, onion, leek, cabbage and bacon in the base of the dish. Arrange the chops in a single layer over the bacon and cover with layers of the remaining vegetables and bacon.

3 Pour in enough of the stock to cover, then bring to the boil over high heat. Reduce the heat, cover, and simmer for 1$^1/_2$ hours, or until the meat is very tender and the sauce is slightly reduced. Season well with salt and freshly ground black pepper and serve sprinkled with the parsley.

INGREDIENTS

1 kg (2 lb) large raw prawns (jumbo shrimp)
100 g (3$^1/_2$ oz) butter
2 large cloves garlic, crushed
1 teaspoon ground cumin
1 teaspoon paprika
1$^1/_2$ teaspoons garam masala
2 tablespoons good-quality ready-made tandoori paste
2 tablespoons tomato paste (purée)
300 ml thick cream
1 teaspoon sugar
$^1/_3$ cup (90 g) plain yoghurt
2 tablespoons chopped fresh coriander (cilantro) leaves
1 tablespoon flaked almonds, toasted

1 Peel and devein the prawns, leaving the tails intact. Melt the butter in a large saucepan over medium heat, then add the garlic, cumin, paprika and 1 teaspoon of the garam masala and cook for 1 minute, or until fragrant. Add the tandoori paste and tomato paste, and cook for a further 2 minutes. Stir in the cream and sugar, then reduce the heat and simmer for 10 minutes, or until the sauce thickens slightly.

2 Add the prawns to the pan and cook for 8–10 minutes, or until they are pink and cooked through. Remove the pan from the heat and stir in the yoghurt, the remaining garam masala and half the coriander. Season.

3 Garnish with the flaked almonds and remaining coriander and serve with steamed rice and lemon wedges.

All our recipes are thoroughly tested in a specially developed test kitchen. Standard metric measuring cups and spoons are used in the development of our recipes. All cup and spoon measurements are level. We have used 60 g (2¼ oz/Grade 3) eggs in all recipes. Sizes of cans vary from manufacturer to manufacturer and between countries – use the can size closest to the one suggested in the recipe.

CONVERSION GUIDE

1 cup = 250 ml (9 fl oz)

1 teaspoon = 5 ml

1 Australian tablespoon = 20 ml (4 teaspoons)

1 UK/US tablespoon = 15 ml (3 teaspoons)

DRY MEASURES

30 g = 1 oz

250 g = 9 oz

500 g = 1 lb 2 oz

LIQUID MEASURES

30 ml = 1 fl oz

125 ml = 4 fl oz

250 ml = 9 fl oz

LINEAR MEASURES

6 mm = ¼ inch

1 cm = ½ inch

2.5 cm = 1 inch

CUP CONVERSIONS – DRY INGREDIENTS

1 cup almonds, slivered whole = 125 g (4½ oz)

1 cup cheese, lightly packed processed cheddar = 155 g (5½ oz)

1 cup wheat flour = 125 g (4½ oz)

1 cup wholemeal flour = 140 g (5 oz)

1 cup minced (ground) meat = 250 g (9 oz)

1 cup pasta shapes = 125 g (4½ oz)

1 cup raisins = 170 g (6 oz)

1 cup rice, short grain, raw = 200 g (7 oz)

1 cup sesame seeds = 160 g (6 oz)

1 cup split peas = 250 g (9 oz)

INTERNATIONAL GLOSSARY

capsicum	sweet bell pepper
chick pea	garbanzo bean
chilli	chile, chili pepper
cornflour	cornstarch
eggplant	aubergine
spring onion	scallion
zucchini	courgette
plain flour	all-purpose flour
prawns	shrimp
minced meat	ground meat

Where temperature ranges are indicated, the lower figure applies to gas ovens, the higher to electric ovens. This allows for the fact that the flame in gas ovens generates a drier heat, which effectively cooks food faster than the moister heat of an electric oven, even if the temperature setting is the same.

	°C	°F	GAS MARK
Very slow	120	250	½
Slow	150	300	2
Mod slow	160	325	3
Moderate	180	350	4
Mod hot	190(g)–210(e)	375–425	5
Hot	200(g)–240(e)	400–475	6
Very hot	230(g)–260(e)	450–525	8

Published in 2006 by Bay Books,
an imprint of Murdoch Books Pty Limited.

ISBN 1-74045-945-8
978-1-74045-945-7

Printed by Sing Cheong Printing Company Ltd.
Printed in China.